COMMUNE OR NOTHING!

COMMUNE OR NOTHING!

Venezuela's Communal Movement and Its Socialist Project

by CHRIS GILBERT

MONTHLY REVIEW PRESS

New York

Library of Congress Cataloging-in-Publication data
available from the publisher.

ISBN paper: 978-1-68590-023-6
ISBN cloth: 978-1-68590-024-3

Typeset in Bulmer MT

MONTHLY REVIEW PRESS, NEW YORK
monthlyreview.org

5 4 3 2 1

Contents

A quienes toman el cielo por asalto en Venezuela
y en otras partes del mundo

Author's Note

Karl Marx wrote that theory becomes a material force when it grips the masses. He should have added that theory usually grips the masses because it connects with ideas, projects, and dreams they have developed themselves. This is what generally happens in revolutions, and it is certainly the case for the idea of the communal project in Venezuela. In 2009, ten years after the Bolivarian Process began, Hugo Chávez proposed the communal path to socialism in a historic television program. That project had solid bases in the thought of Marx and István Mészáros, yet it would have been dead in the water if the idea of replacing a society dominated by the logic of capital with one based on communal relations had not connected with aspirations and values already alive and operating in Venezuelan society.

As it turned out, self-organized communities around the country seized on the communal project, which resonated both with values shaped over the *longue durée* in Venezuela—through its enduring campesino, Indigenous, and Afro-Venezuelan traditions of self-governance—and also with newer practices and principles, such as "participative and protoganistic democracy," that had formed during the course of the revolutionary process.

This book, with its stories, commentary, and reflections, is a testament to the way that theoretical spark—communal socialism posited as an alternative to capital's rule—was able to set fire to a field that had been kindled through numerous efforts over the course of Venezuelan history. The result, documented in what follows, is a powerful if incipient movement that offers hope and lessons for those seeking change around the world.

In researching Venezuela's communal movement, which I have been doing together with Cira Pascual Marquina over the past few years, we received help from numerous individuals. In the first place are the communards in Venezuela who took the time to educate us about the nature of their project. To them, this book is dedicated. At the Observatorio Venezolano Antibloqueo, William Castillo, Blandina Araujo, Abelaicy González, José Silva, Alexandra Stuparic, and Miriam Perdomo made invaluable contributions by facilitating our research travel to different communes in the country and sometimes accompanying the trips. Writer and filmmaker Gerardo Rojas was a fascinating interlocutor regarding the history and challenges of communal construction, who took part in many of these visits to communes. For kindly sharing his manuscript *Chávez lector de Nietzsche* with me, I am grateful to Reinaldo Iturriza. In the course of writing the book, I was encouraged and advised by the brilliant and generous Michael Lebowitz, who sadly passed away just as we were going to press (Rest in power, comrade!). Thanks also to Ashley Hufnagel and Ricardo Vaz who read and commented on parts of the manuscript, and to Erin Clermont, who copy-edited it. Kael Abello of the Utopix collective made the wonderful cover art. Finally, my deep gratitude goes to Michael Yates, Martin Paddio, and Rebecca Manski at Monthly Review Press, for their support of the project and for making its publication possible.

—CARACAS, APRIL 2023

Introduction: Putting the Commune Back into Communism

There is growing awareness in our time that the post-capitalist society can only be made by people as a collective project that is neither automatic nor imposed. This in turn has contributed to a renewed interest in communes on the part of the left. But while communes today may seem to provide people with an alternative way of living and producing, they are not new. In fact, for much of humanity's past, among diverse social groups, the principal means of production was land, and it belonged to people not as individuals but rather to the group, or the commune. In these communities, people's sense of belonging could be profound, so much so that as embedded producers they considered land to be an extension of their lives and even bodies. However, they did so as a group, meaning that the individuals related to the land *by way of* the community.

The same could be said for the relation that the first crafts-people had to their tools and trades: the tools belonged to a community, or to an individual *through the community*. For example, in the Bengali villages that Marx took an interest in, a craftsperson, such as a smith or carpenter, usually possessed the tools of a trade as part of an established role in an agrarian commune, while in much of Europe, there existed guilds that amounted to communities of tradespeople and producers.[1] The epoch of communal production's dominance is long-lasting, for even when original, classless communities gave way, in most places, to pre-capitalist societies divided into classes, the majority of work retained its embedded character. This meant that a "bare worker" was almost unimaginable: a worker separated and stripped from a communal context defined mainly by shared conditions of work.[2]

The profound connectedness of people to their communities and the control they exercised over their shared work conditions meant that only a radical violence could separate them from those contexts. Yet, as we know, that violence occurred wherever capitalism appeared; Marx described the separation with memorable words, as a process "dripping from head to toe, from every pore, with blood and dirt."[3] From that brutal rupture, modern society emerged, along with modern forms of exploitation and modern individualism, and other features that we associate with the capital system.[4] Much was destroyed as a result of this violent process, and much was lost. Nevertheless, there were significant horizons of human development that eventually arose under the social formations of the capital system, formations in which abstract economic relations more than personal ones ruled people's lives.[5] These new horizons were especially important in the sense of breaking down barriers and overcoming (albeit in a highly unequal manner) the limited sets of needs and satisfactions under which people had formerly lived when in traditional communes.[6]

Today, however, there is no denying the destruction of the natural environment and of human beings that the capital system has brought, where all is subordinated to an inexorable process of economic valorization that amounts to a virtual treadmill of senseless expansion. This process, far from abating, presses forward in our time with ever greater aggressiveness, with new forms of capital accumulation that prey on spheres of life previously outside of capitalism's reach. By contrast, communal systems are more sustainable, less destructive and alienating, and, in many senses, more humanly gratifying. For these reasons, they form an attractive reference, which may seem to be an inspiring alternative in the face of the capital system. That said, the communal way of life lies far in the past for most of us, and it was sometimes the locus of traditional forms of oppression.[7] What to do then? What is the solution to our dilemma? What futures can we aspire to at the current crossroads that humanity faces? Are we condemned forever to live with the current alienating, exploiting, and nature-destroying system that has reached across the globe?[8] Or should we try to recover the communal form of production and life?

Hence, our options may seem to be between present-day capitalism and what is, for most people, a historically distant communalism. However, presented as the option of choosing between the undesirable (capitalist progress) and the almost impossible (return), the question is badly posed. In fact, a revolutionary solution to the dire problems that capitalism has brought will not involve rewinding the clock entirely, but rather reaching back with a critical vision to recover those elements of communal systems, especially living and working in communal and classless societies, that can point to a future in which human beings enjoy self-determined, more sustainable, and fuller lives. But it is not only about recovery. The use of the communal form today, its adoption, should take place through a dialectical reappropriation of the past in which modern horizons of personal freedom and cultural diversity are preserved and some of capitalism's technological advances are employed within a democratic approach to production and life that is rational, sustainable, and beneficial to both human beings and the natural environment.

This book is about that complex project of human emancipation and preservation of the Earth system. It is about communal socialism, or modern socialism using the commune as a building block. It looks at that project as it took root in a small corner of the world, in Venezuela, where today, as a result of a process of national liberation that began two decades ago, there is a contemporary effort at socialist construction based on the communal form, taking its lead from important precedents both in Latin American history and in revolutionary theory, especially that of Karl Marx. Specifically, the book tells the story of how the Venezuelan people, along with a remarkable leader named Hugo Chávez, seized on and interpreted the project of advancing toward a better future based on the commune as a socialist building block. The book looks at the steps that Venezuelan communards have taken in our time—first steps for now, taken in very difficult conditions—and the ideas and projects they have developed. It is the belief of many of us, both inside and outside Venezuela's communal movement, that these small steps are of great importance to humanity as a whole.

THE ESSENCE OF THE COMMUNE

Why build a commune? What are the advantages of the communal system? When you visit an urban commune these days in Venezuela, you might encounter various workshops and other spaces for production, or if it's a rural commune there will be fields with crops and maybe livestock. Along with this, there will be meeting spaces and residences that surround the commune. People might seem happier or more relaxed than normal, but perhaps not. Indeed, many people will be engaged in work or leisure activities that are similar to those one sees everywhere in the capitalist world. So, what is the essence of the commune in all of this? In fact, what Bertolt Brecht said about a factory—that, from the outside, you cannot tell much about the real social relations, capitalist or socialist, operating there—applies to what you can see in a Venezuelan commune. The essence of a commune is a new set of social relations, which are usually not immediately visible. The most important of these—and a necessary feature of the communal system, as it existed before and might exist in the future—is directly social labor.

What is directly social labor in this context? Briefly, it means labor activities that are carried out in the name of goals and with methods that the community itself decides. This is not very mysterious, for in today's world there is an ample array of labor activities that are still carried out with a direct interpersonal goal in mind, that is, whose social character is not mediated by commodity exchange. These include much of care work, domestic labor, and subsistence activities—the various forms of work sometimes described as *social reproductive labor*. This kind of labor, despite the oppressive contexts in which it is often carried out, is usually done with the goal of helping or caring for people and not for money or exchange. However, labor that is paid and considered "productive" for the society at large, the more recognized and visible forms of labor, is a different matter. This kind of labor, which is decisive in our society, is not *directly* social at all because, as private production, its social character is mediated by the exchange of commodities. This means that it becomes social *only after* being crystallized in a product that passes through the circuit of exchange, that is, after it acquires the form of value.

The mediation of labor activities and exchange by value-bearing commodities is enough to interrupt labor's directly social character, concealing the laborer behind fetishized commodities, but there is more to the strange circuits of production that operate in our economies. That is because, in our societies, labor power itself has become a commodity, through the wage system. Hence, even if there is much concrete, non-alienated but undervalued and unpaid labor dedicated to reproducing life in our time, this is only half the story. A huge range of labor processes, namely those that incorporate commodified wage labor, involve conditions such as tools, machinery, and technology that are separated from the worker. They are owned and controlled by someone else, while the worker now simply works to earn a living. This scenario overturns centuries of traditional practices, and it results in a situation where not only do work conditions come to confront workers as something alien, separated from them, but even work activities themselves become external, imposed, and threatening to workers.[9] These activities (which become a mere "job") no longer belong to the worker, nor does the product. Moreover, the labor process ceases to be under the worker's control. The inexorable imperative to make profit, which dominates and determines the labor process from beginning to end, means that, in a sense, no one is in control!

A good parable for this condition—one that Marx and Engels refer to in the *Communist Manifesto*—is found in J.W. von Goethe's poem "Der Zauberlehrling," made popular as the "Sorcerer's Apprentice" sequence in Disney's 1940 film *Fantasia*. In Goethe's poem, a bewitched broom, which can be taken to refer to work that is no longer under human control—as in the capital system with its imperative to accumulate—does the work for an apprentice. The magical broom begins to fill bucket after bucket of water. This seems good at first, but the unstoppable and automatic bucket brigade that the apprentice has conjured into being soon leads to dangerous flooding. In our society, we are living in that flood, that debacle. And what we are living is only the beginning of it. The natural conditions for life on the planet are being destroyed and they risk reaching points of no return, as is evident in the reports that scientists regularly develop and diffuse only to have politicians ignore them. Meanwhile the human being—a human being stretched on the rack of alienated labor, making good on the etymological connection between labor and torture so common in Romance languages—risks being carried away by the uncontrollable tide.[10] The formerly "charmed" use of alienated labor, which might once have seemed beneficial and innocent, now shows its dangerous, destructive, and even demonic face.

In sharp contrast, the communal system, as it is being pursued in Venezuela, promises to put the "brooms" back into the hands of the people themselves and their communities. It proposes to restore labor conditions and instruments to freely associated

producers, who will decide how to use and control them—
thereby de-alienating these producers' labor—and at the same
time allow for the liberation of the undervalued, often coerced
work of social reproduction by making it shared and collective.
The most important transformation in the communal system that
is taking shape today in the country, though mainly in the grassroots, is that it would put all labor once again under democratic
and direct social control, since in this new way of producing
there would no longer be labor activities that become social only
post festum, that is, only through the ricochet of products in the
market. The bizarre break between production and consumption
that exists under the capital system, in which commodities make
their daily "leap into the void" of the market as exchange-values,
would be overcome. Production of use-values would be recon-
nected to consumption and real needs, which would become
"communal consumption" for that reason.

In this new society freed from the necessity of producing
exchange-values, reproducing life in its rich and diverse manifes-
tations and the community's well-being would be the priorities,
not capital accumulation. There would be no automatic process
of valorization, no senseless treadmill. Freed from the constraints
of value-production, the society of associated producers—producers brought together in communes of different kinds—could
dispose of time according to self-determined aims, with a view to
expanding individual free time and promoting all-round human
development in a way that is harmonious with the natural environment.[11] Ending the tyranny of value-production would also
allow productive and reproductive or household work to be
equally valued and bring an end to the capital system's historic
separation of these two spheres. These are the merits of the communal format. Moreover, whatever virtues the capital system
had—which mainly consist in the expansion of human horizons
that occurred under its reign—would have to be incorporated
into the new society. Likewise, in the new communal system,
technological innovation and the resulting productivity would

exist in a different, more manageable form. It would be manageable inasmuch as an expansiveness that is uncontrollable or automatic is impossible by definition under a regime of directly social labor.

GENESIS OF THE COMMUNAL PROJECT IN VENEZUELA

In Venezuela, the project of building socialism through a communal system emerged out of a complex historical process. Despite this complexity, it is easy to trace how the first ideals and principles that guided the Bolivarian Revolution when it emerged at the turn of the century were taken up and continued in the subsequent communal project. From the beginning, this political movement defended *participative and protagonistic democracy*, which was expressed in a range of documents (including some from before taking power) and also practices.[12] The latter included massive, direct participation in the Constitutional Assembly of 1999 and subsequent referendums (1999, 2004, 2007), but also the various community organizations Chávez's government promoted that were expressions of popular power. Most notable among these were the community councils that emerged in 2005, along with the Technical Water Forums (Mesas Técnicas de Agua) and Urban Land Committees (Comités de Tierra Urbana), all of them aimed at establishing democratic control from the grassroots.

In the second part of the decade, the Bolivarian Revolution's commitment to participative and protagonistic democracy would continue in different guises, as a regulative ideal, finally issuing into the commune. This occurred through a more or less logical unfolding of the basic principle of democratic self-emancipation. An important step took place in 2006, when the country's project, which had been defined by expanding grassroots democracy and anti-imperialism, now morphed into the project of socialism, which Chávez called "democracy squared." Next, after a brief flirtation with some more top-down models and after the slap in the face the government received in 2007 with the vote against the Constitutional Reform, the country's model became communal socialism—or socialism by way of the commune as a "basic cell." This occurred in 2009, with the Law of Communes being developed a year later. The Law of Communes was in many ways a high-water mark as far as governmental programs and projects were concerned. It was passed in a packet of laws, the *Popular Power Laws*, at a time when Chávez's government, because of the torrential rains and flooding that occurred at the end of 2010, had been granted the power to legislate by decree. The government wasted no time in generating five laws on the themes of popular power, communes, and the communal economy. These laws laid out the basic structural model for Venezuelan communes, as instances of grassroots political and economic democracy, which were to be built by joining community councils and other popular organizations in a zone.

The *Popular Power Laws* were very thorough ones, promulgating communal planning, communal cities, federations of communes, and even the communal state. Most important, they called for a profound transformation of productive relations. Article 12 of the Law of the Communal Economic System described those new relations as: "A production model based on social property, oriented toward eliminating the social division of labor that is typical of the capitalist model." The article also made clear the overall goal: "The socialist production model is aimed at satisfying the growing needs of the population, through new forms of creation and appropriation." These laws left little to be desired as far as the main features of socialist communes are concerned: they ratified the importance of non-alienated work, collective property, production focused on use-values, and satisfying the expanding needs of the population while addressing the question of social use of the economic surplus. The laws also had special provisions for Indigenous communes. These vanguard laws, which had their roots in the movement's long-standing commitment to participative, grassroots democracy, even pointed to an overcoming or transformation of the state, as is indicated not only by the implicit class position of the project of building socialism from below, but also by their references to a future "communal state."

To some it might seem strange that one would try to "legislate revolution" in this way, and indeed the whole question connects with the complex relation between state power and social revolution that will come up at various points in this book. However, the *Popular Power Laws* were different from most laws that operate in capitalist states in that they were aimed at empowering those from below, who would therefore have to assume responsibility for the laws and bring them to realization. It was precisely for this reason that, after the communal path was made official, Chávez began his usual process of persuading people to participate in and deepen the revolution from the bully pulpit he had developed as the revolution's "communicator in chief." Chávez had done so before with cooperatives and community councils, along with other government initiatives. Now, however, his discursive work took the form of explaining and encouraging people to go forward and build communes. He explained most features of the communal project very carefully in the television program *Aló Presidente Teórico No. 1*. Chávez said there that the commune would be a "heroic construction" carried out by the masses and also the place where socialism would be born. He subsequently outlined the ethical, economic, and political dimensions of the project, while warning about the importance of communes maintaining autonomy from the newly founded PSUV party (United Socialist Party of Venezuela). The communal project as a strategic horizon would be ratified over the upcoming years in various discourses and writings, even if fewer steps were taken on the ground than could have been desired. The project received its most significant endorsement in Chávez's last important speech, *Strike at the Helm*, where the president articulated the slogan that has since become the rallying cry of the country's communal movement: "Commune or Nothing!"[13]

Vicissitudes of the Communal Project

The process by which Venezuela arrived at communal socialism as a societal project can be presented, as we have done just now, according to a linear, step-by-step narrative: it can be seen as the logical upshot of a revolutionary process and its principles, mainly grassroots democracy, which reached their organic culmination in the project of communal socialism. However, to do so risks ignoring some notable obstacles and vicissitudes that the communal project underwent. These are of various kinds and include widespread resistance among intellectuals (whose class commitments are evident in their ongoing practice of prioritizing Venezuela's oil reserves rather than its socialism as the bone of contention with imperialism). On top of this, there was a complicated geopolitical context in the continent, with the progressive governments that were once Venezuela's allies losing ground in the face of imperialism's containment tactics, especially the coups the United States promoted in Honduras in 2009 and Paraguay in 2012. These aggressions worked to impede the advance of progressive governments in the region in what has come to be known as the "Pink Tide." This adverse geopolitical situation may go some way to explaining why Chávez, in an apparently contradictory way, deployed so much of the Venezuelan state's resources, from 2010 to his death, in essentially social relief projects such as the Great Housing Mission, even as he talked about communal socialism.

However, the most important vicissitude the communal project has faced has been served up to it not by foot-dragging intellectuals or the destabilizing hand of imperialism, but by the project's reception in the masses themselves. This is so much so that the overarching story of Venezuelan communes, in concrete terms, is not a linear one but rather a trajectory that follows a kind of sine wave, dipping to almost zero at one point before rising up at a later time. That is to say, when Chávez launched the idea of making communes in 2009, though there were some notable exceptions, the project generally got little traction in the masses. The overall conjuncture, because of the oil-stoked abundance during the commodity super-cycle that was occurring then, was adverse to the communal project and actually favored the project of "assistentialist" social democracy or the aspiration to build state socialism. The general mood was something like this: Why make the sacrifices of a difficult project of building communes when the oil profits were abundant enough to pay off social debt and even solve the riddle of primitive socialist accumulation that, for example, Yevgeni Preobrazhensky and Nicolai Bukharin debated a hundred years ago in a state socialist context? This meant that Chávez's idea of communal socialism was an "untimely" one, to use Nietzsche's phrase, and it only found a fertile context at a later date, at a time he could not foresee. That time came only after Chávez's death, and well after the economy had taken a sharp downturn, which put the Venezuelan people through one of the worst trials by fire ever in Latin American history.

After Chávez died, the new government led by Chávez's named successor, Nicolás Maduro, faced severe economic crisis and heightened imperialist assault expressed in cruel sanctions and various coup attempts. The government responded with overt pragmatism. It pursued an essentially capitalist path of least resistance that meant turning away from socialism, and even grassroots democracy, and *a fortiori* putting the commune on the furthest of back burners. Price controls were eliminated, real wages reduced, and social programs defunded. Now, between imperialist attacks, economic downturn, and internally imposed shock therapy the wonderful abundance that Venezuelans had lived through in the first decade of the century dissipated like morning haze when the sun rises. It was the worst of times: a moment when the average Venezuelan lost 22 pounds, desperate emigration destroyed families, and the government's ironfisted attitude toward hunger-driven misdemeanors left thousands of youths dead in the barrios. Yet in this extremely bleak situation,

the communal ideal began to shine again. Quietly and unbeknownst to most urban residents and to navel-gazing bureaucrats,
the communal project had been assumed by small groups of
people around the country not only as a solution to the problems
they faced, but also as a way of restoring Chavismo to what they
understood to be its original path and project.

That meant that the worst of times was also the best of times—
for socialism and the communes at least! It was the time when the
rural El Maizal Commune began to seize land in Lara State, when
the Andean Che Guevara Commune began to buckle down and
recover cooperative coffee growing and processing in its fertile
hillsides, and the flagship urban commune El Panal set about
expanding by building *"panalito"* modules throughout the west
of Caracas. In effect, an idea that had fallen on sterile ground
when originally proposed now began to take root. There was a
small but growing group of robust communes in the country and
a much wider web of communal projects that were taking their
first steps. Moreover, they had the objective of going further.

Cira Pascual Marquina and I, residents in Venezuela and participants in the Bolivarian Process since 2006, tried to capture
the spirit of this moment in our 2020 book *Venezuela, the Present
as Struggle*, which documents how a kind of consensus emerged
in the grassroots regarding a Left solution to the country's crisis.
Through numerous interviews carried out in 2018–19, we were
able to ascertain how the Chavista socialist project, far from disappearing during the crisis, had simply burrowed underground;
it had survived in the masses. The ideals of popular power,
participative and protagonistic democracy, and also communal
socialism, were maintained in the grassroots. The "practical-
minded" government might have backburnered these projects,
but the masses had not. Self-critically, we realized that we too had
not fully understood the importance of the commune, both as a
project and a reality operating in the grassroots and were therefore not immune to the myopia of the progressive intellectuals
mentioned above.

In response, we began to make up for lost time with a crash course on the communes as they exist and operate around the country. This new book, *Commune or Nothing!*, is in great measure both a reflection of this process of self-education and an effort to make it available to others. Our first attempt to really get to know the country's communes was a trip to El Maizal Commune, in Lara State, which is chronicled in chapter 1 of this book. To our pleasant surprise, we saw that the main Chavista ideals and a revolutionary horizon, though more or less abandoned in official spheres, were alive and well in this rural redoubt. A light bulb turned on, spurring a desire to go on investigating. Next was a revelatory trip to the Che Guevara Commune in the foothills of the Venezuelan Andes, which is presented in chapter 3. Then came an investigation of three communes—Luisa Cáceres, Monte Sinaí, and Cinco Fortalezas—in eastern Venezuela (chapter 5) and participation in the foundational congress of the nascent Communard Union (chapter 6). Subsequently, we visited the self-managed Indorca metallurgy workshop in Bolívar State, which is not technically a commune but operates with much the same spirit and has a volunteer brigade, the Productive Workers Army, that has worked with several communes (chapter 7). Last but not least, we investigated El Panal Commune, which is right under our noses at just a few metro stops from where we live in Caracas (chapter 8).

By the time the investigation was coming to a provisional close, a happy coincidence would have it that a new interest in the communes was being widely felt among Venezuelan intellectuals, grassroots leaders, and even the government itself. In a surprising about-face, President Maduro called for 2023 to be the "year of the communes" and insisted that "everything that needed to be changed would be changed." Clearly, there was a new wind blowing: a new optimism and a widely felt sense that the communal project was something emergent that was perhaps capable of re-hegemonizing the Bolivarian Process and redirecting it to socialism. Future readers (though not too far in the future since

Venezuelan history moves so fast!) will be able to judge for themselves whether this hope, which is expressed so frequently in
these pages, has come to pass and brought with it both a change
of power relations in the country's governmental spheres and a
shift toward socialism in the economy.

MARX AND COMMUNES

Marx famously wrote that communism was not an ideal to be
imposed on reality, but rather "the *real* movement that abolished
the present state of things." He meant by that the real social and
historical movement, which he next clarified as resulting "from
conditions now in existence."[14] It is clear that the real historical
movement of emancipation has led Venezuelan revolutionaries
along the tortuous path sketched above to the commune as a
building block of socialism. Nevertheless, the commune's role in
socialism also has solid theoretical bases in revolutionary theory.
If chapter 2 of this book combines a look at the long roots of
the Venezuelan communal system in the region's Indigenous,
Maroon, and peasant communities, along with its basis in Latin
American Marxism, then chapter 4 explores some of the project's
underpinnings in recent Marxian theory. However, the commune
also played a central role in the thought of Marx himself, though
its centrality has long been underrecognized. This is so much
so that much of what the Venezuelan people did in the early
twenty-first century was simply to restore Marxism to its original
proposals, though these were mostly buried under the detritus of
false doctrine.
    This recovery of original Marxism that happened in
Venezuela—which I like to call *putting the commune back into
communism*—has to do with both the commune as the organizational format or building block of socialism and the democratic,
self-organized means of getting there.[15] Regarding the format,
many have commented on Marx's reticence about the future
emancipated society that could replace capitalism. Various

explanations have been given, such as Marx's lack of time or
the underdeveloped nature of the capitalism he studied. It is
clearly the case that one cannot find in Marx's work a thorough
description of socialist or communist society. Commentators
are undoubtedly correct about this. Still, just as salient as this
absence is the remarkable lack of commentary about the lines
that actually do appear—and do so repeatedly—in Marx's writing about a society of "freely associated producers" in such
central works as the *Communist Manifesto* and *Capital.* These
are clearly references to the post-capitalist, emancipated society
that he envisioned and felt was immanent in the existing one. In
the *Communist Manifesto*, Marx and Engels project a society,
based on association, in which "the free development of each is
the condition for the development of all," while no less than eight
times does Marx refer to *freely associated producers* or variations
on that phrase in the three volumes of *Capital.*[16] What kind of
post-capitalist society is being referred to here? "Freely associated producers" or "freely associated people"[17] is not an empty
phrase or mere revolutionary rhetoric—that is, words that sound
good and maybe inspire people to struggle. First of all, it refers
to how those who actually produce (not their bosses, whether
private executives or state bureaucrats) must associate *themselves*
(not, therefore, have abstract collectivization imposed on them).
Further, it projects a situation where these producers operate as
free and self-determined agents. This means that their activities
are not determined by economic forces or the law of value. Nor
are they controlled by some external agency, either patriarchal or
paternalistic, or even by an externally imposed production plan.
Hence, the phrase is an almost undeniable reference to producers being organized in communes. Where else can one produce
in free association and rule oneself? Where else can useful and
enjoyable activities be coordinated without being mediated by
the exchange of things?

    These references to freely associated production resonate with
Marx's claims in his 1857–58 *Grundrisse* manuscript (which is

in some ways his most comprehensive work). There, Marx not only consistently describes community production as the original condition for historical development—"Communal property [is] the point of departure of all cultured [sic] peoples," he writes—but he comes full circle and declares it to be the goal. This is evident when Marx affirms that "perfection is found in voluntary associations" and refers to the new society that could emerge after capitalism as one with "a communal character of production" where there is an "exchange of . . . activities determined by communal needs and purposes."[18] Further evidence for Marx's wagering on the commune comes from how he not only supported the Paris Commune of 1871 but pronounced it to be "the political form at last discovered under which to work out the economical emancipation of labour."[19] Almost ten years later and near the end of his life, Marx ratified the possibility of using the peasant commune, as it persisted in the Russian countryside, as a springboard for socialist development in his much-celebrated letter and drafts to Vera Zasulich (see chapter 2).

So much, then, for the relevance of the commune to the project of building the post-capitalist society. It is clearly a format that, if employed consciously and in dialogue with modern development, Marx thought could transform existing social relations from bottom to top, thereby building socialism. What about the methods of organization used to build communes? Is socialist emancipation the task of some enlightened group, institution, or individual, who might impose their projects on the passive masses? As is well known, but seemingly just as easily forgotten, this was an idea that Marx rejected in the utopian socialists from the beginning and also manifested in his dislike of Ferdinand Lassalle's state-friendly and leader-centric approach to socialism.[20] Marx always held that the human being was the subject and not the predicate of change and therefore defended self-emancipation.

Nevertheless, a kind of substitutionist vanguardism as a means for socialist construction—even vanguardism with an authoritarian turn—has persisted as a model up to the present. The story of twentieth-century socialism is largely one of how a state-party vanguardism, misbranded as Leninism, was consolidated (through a complicated process in which no one individual can be blamed) as socialist orthodoxy. Yet this "orthodoxy," essentially the idea that the state and party can conduct the socialist project, which is in turn conceived as a command economy with the masses cast in the role of beneficiaries, is outright revisionism. It replicates the subject-predicate inversion that Marx opposed, and results in no more than another form of extracting surplus labor from above in an economy in which the labor processes are not controlled by direct producers. Marx from the beginning was committed to the conscious, self-emancipation of the working class, and he did so not for sentimental reasons but because anything else was a contradiction in terms when the issue is people *becoming full and active subjects*. Self-emancipation was a paradigm that Marx put forth first at age twenty-five in a letter to Arnold Ruge (1843), and he never abandoned it.[21]

This means that when the Venezuelan people—who for reasons of history have long been committed to grassroots democracy, and have rebelled on numerous occasions in its name[22]—turned to the communal paradigm and proposed to build their communes via a process of self-emancipation, with themselves as protagonists, they were simply recovering this original but repeatedly sidelined socialist and Marxist idea as part of their ongoing project of emancipation through profoundly democratic means. Experience and study had taught them that the overall social metabolism was the most important thing to change, and only by altering it under the aegis of a transformed state apparatus could they eventually overcome the whole capital system. Doing so would be no easy task, and yet a people who had such a long trajectory of rebellion—with Venezuelans serving as the vanguard of the independence struggle two hundred years ago and being engaged in a more or less constant state of social insurgency ever since—were willing to take up the gauntlet. They faced the challenge in the spirit of a do-or-die struggle, which came to be known as the battle for their "Second and Final Independence."

EXISTENTIAL OPTIONS

The idea of an all-or-nothing existential struggle for socialism is expressed in the slogan that was chosen as the title for this work: *Commune or Nothing!* That slogan is the main battle cry of Venezuela's communal movement today, and one hears it constantly in the mouths of communard militants and leaders. State officials, too, must appeal to it whenever they attempt to reach out to the communal movement. The phrase has important precedents in both the Cuban slogan *¡Patria o Muerte!* (Country or Death!) and in Rosa Luxemburg's *Socialism or Barbarism*, with which it resonates because it juxtaposes two polar opposites as alternatives. In the history of the Bolivarian Process, one can trace how heroic slogans of this kind, slogans that clearly expressed the existential alternatives at stake in the project of emancipation, were used early on, then faded away, only to be recovered in this new slogan. That is to say, for the first half-decade or so of the Bolivarian Process, *¡Patria o Muerte!* and *Independence, Socialism, or Death!* circulated widely. Then around 2007 came a time of retreat, when the overall tone of the process shifted to a more affirmative mode, and the dominant slogans became ones like *Viviremos y Venceremos* (We Will Live and We Will Win), and *Patria, Socialismo y Vida* (Country, Socialism, and Life). In effect, negation, an important part of Marxian dialectics and its revolutionary worldview, had been erased from the Bolivarian Process's imaginary, as had the possibility expressed in the *Communist Manifesto*—and truer than ever in our time— that the outcome of class struggle could be mutual destruction instead of one class defeating the other.

Yet there is more to tell here. The story of how Chávez abandoned these more affirmative and bland slogans and then finally returned, with the enunciation of *Commune or Nothing!*, to a vision that accounted for the true nature of the challenges and risks facing humanity, has been recovered in an investigation by Venezuelan intellectual Reinaldo Iturriza.[23] The period he looks at is Chávez's last years of life which were marked by the awareness that he had contracted an aggressive cancer, imbuing him with a sense of urgency. Over the course of his last year, Chávez became aware that the communal project had not really taken root in a concrete way in the masses, nor had it been embraced fully by his ministerial cabinet. During his last cabinet meeting, in October 2012, this is what made Chávez angrily ask his ministers the pointed questions: "Where is the commune?" and "Where are these so-called communes in construction?" The discourse he gave in that meeting, which became known as *Golpe de Timón* (Strike at the Helm), constitutes the one and only moment where Chávez would say "Commune or Nothing!" The phrase is not only important because Chávez thought of it, but also because it struck home and later went viral.

The backstory that Iturriza has uncovered is that Chávez had been reading Friedrich Nietzsche during his illness: the sarcoma that was first discovered in 2011. As Iturriza points out, Chávez read Nietzsche in a very personal way, with a particular interest in the figure of the Child that appears in *Thus Spake Zarathustra*, who as a creative spirit is meant to supersede the Camel (a beast of burden) and the Lion (which stands for conflict and overcoming). However, Chávez was also fascinated by the concept of nihilism, the existential option that Nietzsche sometimes describes as *willing nothing*. As luck would have it, Chávez had attended a military event in January 2011, where he heard an officer use the phrase, "Independence or Nothing," attributing it to Bolívar. Hearing these words of Bolívar's made something click in the President. Chávez, who knew the history of the independence like the back of his hand, was taken aback that he had never heard the slogan before. He started to incorporate *Independence or Nothing!* as a slogan in his speeches and simultaneously began to identify his contender in the presidential elections of 2012, Henrique Capriles, and the right-wing opposition more generally, with *nothing* (*la nada*)—that is, with the nihilistic option and with the abyss.

Chávez's identifying the opposition with a nihilistic abyss was because he felt that an opposition government would leave the country with no future. He made this clear when saying that the opposition "represented what is called nihilism, nothing, they are the negation of everything."[24] The claim that Venezuela was involved in an existential struggle, in which the whole of humanity and its future was at stake, was latent in Chávez's speeches and thinking throughout that last year. Implicitly, advancing toward socialism by way of the commune, the project he had proposed three years earlier, came to be understood as the only alternative to the nihilistic abyss. However, it was only once, in the *Golpe de Timón* speech, that Chávez actually riffed on Bolívar's phrase to obtain the "Commune or Nothing!" slogan. It was a unique utterance, but one heard around the world. With this slogan, which connects the history of socialism with that of independence, touching along the way upon existential philosophy, Chávez wove together the aspiration of national liberation with the socialist project and the future of humanity. The commune was the Archimedean point or crossroads where all of it came together.

A Date with History

A word should be said about Romanticism which, in the sense of a past-oriented worldview, is clearly present in Venezuela's communal project, with its significant nods toward the idea of reappropriating a historically sidelined way of life, specifically the communal form of social organization, in present-day circumstances. This book reflects that project in both its content and style. Indeed, in the pages that follow, I frequently allude to breaches or jumps in the continuum of time, straying far from the model of Cartesian linearity and the progressive view of history. This approach, call it *revolutionary romanticism*, which is fundamental to the Venezuelan practice of socialist construction, needs to be distinguished both from the *naive romanticism* that dreams of the "simple life" and from the *reactionary romanticism* that approaches the past uncritically while rejecting the emancipatory horizons and aspirations that emerged under modernity (admittedly, aspirations that usually remain unfulfilled). This approach to the past could seem exotic, if it were not so much a part of popular consciousness in Venezuela. In fact, both Chávez and the wider militancy of the Bolivarian Process relied on a conception of time that is made up of strange twists and turns that, like wormholes, connect past and present struggles. In this worldview, an opening in the present could lead us to a gold mine of the past, from which a revolutionary vein of ideas and a stream of living memory could emerge from the catacombs of history and legend into a revolutionary present. This is what Chávez did with historical personages such as Simón Bolívar, Manuela Sáenz, Ezequiel Zamora, Juana "La Avanzadora" Ramírez, Simón Rodríguez (Samuel Robinson), and others that make up Venezuela's combative past. These figures made their "tiger's leap," to use the phrase of revolutionary romantic Walter Benjamin, into the twenty-first century. The idea was to open a space of untold possibilities: a *Jetztzeit* or moment of revolutionary praxis, through which an incomplete historical project could take life and move forward in the present.[25]

Something similar could be said of the idea of the commune. It is clearly part of a past that is not too distant for much of Venezuela, where significant numbers of Indigenous people live even now in communal form, while elements of African, Indigenous, and peasant communal culture survive, though sometimes only latently, in the society. These cultures and traditions, past and present, embody a more sustainable, less alienated, and in many ways freer mode of living and producing. This means that, either as present-day practices or latent memories, such communal traditions and modes of life can and should be made to form part of commune-building today. They have a central role to play in the project of a revolutionary opening onto the future that is partly inspired by them. At the same time, the nature of the revolutionary reappropriation of the communal model must be, as Marx constantly insisted right up through his last writings, one that involves not a mere return to the traditional or historical commune, as some Russian populists proposed in the nineteenth century, but the critical *use* and *adaptation* of it in the present-day modern context. Most especially, the contemporary use of the commune must be one that allows for developing "free individuality," the basis of which was laid through the expansion of needs, aspirations, and satisfactions that emerged as possibilities over the course of modern class struggle.

Fortunately, this approach is basic to the thinking of Venezuelan communards. For example, when we encounter communard leader Robert Longa in the upcoming pages, he will emphasize that his organization, in constructing El Panal, is "adapting the commune, updating and actualizing it for present circumstances." This is important, among other reasons, because oppressive power relations, including patriarchal, racial, cis-heteronormative, and caste-based forms of domination, were sometimes part of the fabric of historical communes and the traditional societies where they existed. Communal socialism cannot accept this. It must seek complete emancipation. The left has a mixed track record on these issues, and it would be unacceptable for communal socialism to repeat the errors of twentieth-century socialism by failing to overcome the range of oppressions that form part of the capital system, even if they preceded it. Correctly understood, the legacy of the varied projects that composed the short century of really existing socialism is that they were not *too* radical, but *not radical enough*, insofar as they did not end such oppressions or made the empty gesture of postponing their overcoming to some later stage.

On a superficial level, communal socialism risks being no

exception to this historical tendency because of the patriarchal and other kinds of oppressive social relations that were built into many historical communes and communities. Indeed, the communal form, as a basic building block for socialism, runs the risk of preserving such injustices if it is appropriated in a *reactionary* way. However, it is just as true that communes, if appropriated in a *revolutionary* way, have the potential to abolish the whole gamut of social oppressions. They in fact hold the promise of building a stronger, more radical and more emancipatory socialism. The reason for this is that the communal form, precisely because it embraces the totality of social existence and proposes to (re)integrate productive and reproductive activities into a democratically organized whole, has the potential to transform the full range of social relations that exist in our society and thus eradicate the entire constellation of oppressions—including sexual, gender, racial, colonial, and political oppression—that together with economic exploitation make up today's patriarchal racial capitalism.

In a basic sense, this emancipatory promise has to do with how communal socialism, through the radical transformations that issue from overcoming the straitjacket of value production, permits us to avoid the typical limitations of historical socialism. Too often the socialist project was reduced to a scenario in which (male) wage laborers combated exploitation, essentially seeking a fairer distribution of wealth, while domestic relations and the forms of oppression that exist in that sphere were left intact. Historical socialism had that crucial limitation: it allowed household labor and other social reproductive activities—labor that has generally fallen on women and racialized people from at least the mid-nineteenth century forward—to be bracketed off by mainstream socialist discourse and practice. As Marxist feminists such as Margaret Benston and Lise Vogel have shown, this approach overlooks how, in a profound and structural sense, oppression in the domestic sphere supports the totality of the system through capitalism's externalizing of reproductive labor, the work that reproduces labor power, into a separate but connected sphere.[26]

By contrast, the communal model, when assumed in revolutionary projects today, has the potential to disallow such a division. This is because the revolutionary commune, through its cohesive approach to work and life and its integrating of communal consumption with communal production, makes this kind of division and bracketing off impossible. The revolutionary commune means emancipation for all or none!

However, it should go without saying that realizing this potential depends on the socialist commune being a *construction*—a heroic one at that—not merely an inheritance of preexisting communal relations that are themselves sometimes tainted by patriarchal and other forms of oppression. A modern socialist commune has to be shaped by the emancipatory projects expressed in powerful social movements in our time: prominent among these being feminism, LGBTQIA+ movements, and anti-racism. In fact, it follows from socialist communes being expressions of *freely* associated labor that they will be feminist, anti-racist, and welcoming of gender diversity. In Venezuela, this is borne out by the concrete practice of commune building in the country for, as will be noted in the pages that follow, its communes provide spaces where relations and identities are in constant construction, and women and members of the country's Black and Brown majority population are the main protagonists in the project. There has been a turning of tables, if still incomplete, of existing power relations, while one also sees how reproductive work has begun to be more fully socialized, public, and shared in the communes, though generally in a more spontaneous than planned manner.

LEARNING ALONG THE WAY

This isn't a book about explaining the communes from an all-knowing perspective. Doing so would be impossible given the nature of its object of study. Socialist construction, which is an ongoing process in Venezuela, is always something that necessitates thinking along the way and working things out downstream.

Likewise, charting its moving targets requires feedback based on a self-critical assimilation of experiences, drawing on both errors and partial successes. Marx himself said that the educator needs to be educated, and he thought that would happen through revolutionary praxis. This Marxist principle applies to Venezuela today, where commune-building as revolutionary practice is nothing if not a process of self-education, and it makes sense that learning and writing about communes would have some of the same character. For that reason, what I propose to do in the pages that follow is mostly to accompany the reader in a process of discovery that in some way parallels the open-ended process of construction that Venezuelan revolutionaries are still working their way through today.

Reality, especially when human praxis is involved, consists of processes that are complex, multilevel, and dialectical, and so must be its reflection. In that spirit, the chapters of this book, some of the preliminary versions of which were published as independent essays, try to weave together theory and observation in the tradition of materialism as expressed not only by Marx and Engels in such marvelous works as *The Eighteenth Brumaire of Louis Bonaparte* and *The Condition of the Working Class in England,* but also William Hinton's books, *Fanshen* and *Shenfan*, which document the Chinese revolution on the level of village life, to mention some very diverse but real sources of inspiration. The idea is to have parallel threads of discourse—such as human stories, economic and political analysis, and even geography—that complement and enrich each other. For the most part, the "truths" or conclusions that the book deals with are not presented beforehand but rather discovered along the way in a process that readers can accompany. This means that the best arguments one will encounter in the following pages are *concrete realities,* not *a priori* demonstrations.

Here we will learn from what has been done and what is being done—often on a small scale and in the face of many challenges— in communal experiments that are necessarily imperfect because they carry the baggage of the past with them, a baggage that will only be left behind with time and self-critical practice. There are hundreds of active communes that exist in Venezuela, but instead of approaching the subject in terms of generalities, we will attempt to penetrate the topic of communal construction by focusing in depth on just a handful of communes, either because they are the most developed and advanced ones or are representative for some other reason. The idea is to open a window on what is happening on the ground in a concrete sense. Hence, we will get a front-row seat on learning processes, but we won't have definitive or final answers that neither the communards themselves, nor the studious and inventive Chávez who inspired them, had either. This is about learning and accompanying a movement characterized by the diversity of its elements and its decentralized nature. Perhaps that is why I found the chronicle to be the most apt literary form to approach the subject in the chapters that deal with specific communes. The chronicle format also allowed me to capture another important reality: that the investigation and writing of this book was carried out in the middle of a pandemic and severe economic crisis, with the U.S. sanctions making life extremely difficult for Venezuelans and, almost needless to say, making travel difficult for investigators.

Finally, I should point out that there is some inevitable ambiguity in the authorial voice used throughout the book. Sometimes "we" is used and sometimes "I," while the authorship of many ideas or appreciations seems to emerge from the spaces between individuals, whether communard or investigator, questioner or respondent. On one level, this can be explained because the subject that was learning and assimilating the experiences was a collective one. The investigative trips that took me to different communes in Venezuela's vast territory over the course of two years were always group undertakings, while many of the observations presented in the book were debated and reflected upon with friends and colleagues. By far the most important of these interlocutors, who was a constant presence in the investigation

and writing of this work, is Cira Pascual Marquina, who contributed to its framing and production immeasurably. On another
level, the slippage between a plural and singular first-person voice
used in the book and the ambiguities that result can function as a
stand-in for the communal subject, the open-ended and expanding subject of change so necessary for our time. It can remind us
that neither a communist nor a communard is ever alone.

1

Red Current, Pink Tide: El Maizal Commune

In 2018, gruesome images of people stoning cattle began to circulate through Venezuela's social networks. The videos came from the countryside and showed people, driven by hunger and destitute, desperately solving their predicament by killing cattle and butchering them in the fields. Venezuela's city dwellers were struck with horror, but they also understood the situation. The crisis and the sanctions were bearing down hard on everyone. The average Venezuelan had lost twenty pounds, clothes hung loose on most people, and medicines were in short supply. It was hardly surprising, then, that the country's poorest were not going to sit around and starve, but rather chose to take matters into their own hands. At least they would be less hungry for a few nights.

At about the same time, in the center-west of the country, a group of seasoned militants from El Maizal Commune began to take stock of the situation in the crisis-ridden country. They were determined to act neither in terms of individual solutions nor to remain passive in the face of the challenge. As their main asset, they ran a midsized communal farm inaugurated shortly after president Hugo Chávez sent out the call to form communes in

2009. The farm had once been in private hands, but the tables were now turned, and it currently served some eight thousand people from twenty *consejos comunales*. The commune's charismatic leader, Ángel Prado, had once worked as a security guard on the land when it was private property.

With so many mouths to feed, El Maizal Commune's leaders knew that they had to strike out in a new direction. "We evaluated the situation," Prado explains to our group visiting from Caracas, "and opted to go on the offensive." They were inspired by Cuban ingenuity and resistance in the face of its sixty-year blockade, especially the island's ability to maintain its population thriving despite sanctions and threats. "We thought, let's apply Fidel's formula. Let's go on the offensive. . . . If having a means of production—say a herd of cattle, a corn field, or some other productive project—could provide us with the economic resources needed to overcome the crisis, then we'll take it!"

The following year, the communards quickly moved to occupy a neighboring pig farm that had once been in the state's hands but had fallen into disuse. They also took over a nearby abandoned university campus. It was all done with careful preparation, mobilizing workers from both locations and working with the neighbors. The newly acquired land and facilities were put under El Maizal's scheme of social property: sharing with the community, internal democracy, and leadership that is answerable to the people. The commune's new assets were immediately set working to produce meat, cheese, and farmed fish. That is how El Maizal grew and prospered during the worst of times in Venezuela, becoming a symbol of resistance and a socialist vanguard in a country where, for most people, the only task is to survive.

A Region with Historical Injustices

It is the summer of 2021, and a group of us from Caracas are traveling to Simón Planas township, where El Maizal Commune is located. We are doing so in an effort to catch up with the communal projects that are developing in the country. These days, Venezuela's vast rural hinterland evokes a forgotten episode in a magical realist novel. Because of the crisis and the gas shortages, adults move around on children's bicycles that the government gave away as Christmas gifts a few years ago. The roadways are full of big human forms hunched over those tiny-wheeled contraptions. They pedal hastily and recall circus clowns. All of this may appear amusing to an outsider, but these people's aims are dead serious: to get to work, see the doctor, or carry out some other necessary errand.

The land here is green and, at this time of year, luxuriant. Nearby mountains collect water that drains into a large valley opening onto the threshold of Venezuela's giant plains region. Important aquifers lie beneath the soil. Just to the north are the mysterious lands of Yaracuy that were much valued by Indigenous people for their year-round fertility. The main highway here leads in forty minutes to Barquisimeto, Venezuela's musical center. However, the melodies of that city, which are strummed on small guitars, give way in this valley to the sounds of *llanero* music, played on harps and full of improvised social content. The lyrics speak of the harsh realities of campesino life and often rail against landlords and the rich.

Because of its fertility and proximity to Venezuela's highly populated central region, this land was long sought after and fought over. After violently expropriating the territory from Indigenous people, a rural oligarchy set up shop, immortalizing themselves in the town and township names. By contrast, ordinary people in Simón Planas led scratch existences as peons on the haciendas of the rich. Until the Bolivarian Revolution, they spent their barely visible lives huddled in villages on the margins of thriving cattle and corn businesses. The contrast was and is shocking. Even now, Simón Planas is home to one of the biggest, most lucrative private slaughterhouses in South America. Just next to it is a huge rum-making complex that exports luxury drinks to Europe.

A Socialist Holdout

One of the clown-cyclists is pedaling his way into the commune. We follow in our van as he turns into the driveway. At the entrance of El Maizal is a large billboard announcing the commune. It reads "Commune or Nothing!" and shows Chávez and Nicolás Maduro on horseback, with the former out in front and the latter hustling to catch up. Soon we arrive to the main cluster of farm buildings. This is no hippie commune: a heavy machinery shed lies off to one side on the right; a noisy corn flour processing unit rises up not far from it; a big cattle-tending complex, with spaces for feeding, washing, and veterinary work, stretches out to the left. All the buildings bear names from the heroic Latin American revolutionary tradition: Camilo Torres (Colombian priest turned guerrillero), Argimiro Gabaldón (Venezuelan revolutionary leader), and Camilo Cienfuegos (martyred Cuban rebel). Tractors are constantly refilling with fertilizer and heading out to the fields, which extend in all directions from the busy rural headquarters.

We are met by Windely Matos, a veteran communard and Prado's right-hand man. With typical Venezuelan no-holds-barred humor, he is usually referred to here as the "Messiah," because of his ability to solve all kinds of problems. As we listen to him explain how things work in El Maizal, we begin to realize how much this commune is like a time machine. The words that once circulated in the Chavista movement's heyday—terms like *solidarity*, *sovereignty*, and even *socialism*—but have since become mostly rhetoric in the official discourse in the cities, are fully meaningful in this rural commune combining production with social experiment.

"El Maizal is living proof that Chávez wasn't mistaken in wagering on the commune," Matos tells us. As if to explain what we have before our eyes, he goes on: "El Maizal shows that the commune is the only way to really satisfy the needs of the *pueblo* and build socialism. . . . For us, Chávez's project is alive, and we will defend and honor it with our lives." Here, among farm machinery, noisome chemicals, and the loud drone of grain-processing machines, his words are credible because they connect with a transformed reality. Far away from well-dressed and overfed bureaucrats, this communard's hopefulness also recalls the spirited attitude of the early Chavista mobilizations.

Matos is keenly aware of the practical problem-solving required to keep a real movement alive. This is his strong suit. The U.S. sanctions are one of the main obstacles to the commune's progress (to say nothing of the well-being of the rest of Venezuelans). Cruel and pointless measures that restrict commerce in everything from fuel to medicine, these sanctions have struck hard against both rural and urban life in Venezuela. One of the commune's survival strategies has been to diversify its economy by incorporating the area's small producers into its network. The commune gives them credits and material support. They, in turn, cultivate what Matos calls "war crops": native beans, yuca, and sorghum. The small producers will later repay the commune with a part of their harvest.

Another huge problem is the local bourgeoisie who harass the commune, while regional bureaucrats too often side with them. The Messiah, however, is unfazed by the opposition put up by regional authorities. "It's well known that here, in this territory, there are two poles of Chavismo. There is a Chavista tendency in the local government that throws up all kinds of obstacles to communal development. Actually, it is not just obstacles," he acknowledges, "sometimes it's plain sabotage." Matos takes heart because he believes that Chávez foresaw such resistance to his plans. Moreover, he tells us how El Maizal has hatched a new strategy in their ongoing battle against the reformist bureaucracy. They will send their main spokesperson, Ángel Prado, to compete for the position of mayor in the upcoming regional elections. Musing about this scenario, I can't suppress the thought that the "Messiah" in this commune—inverting biblical tradition—is announcing the plans of the Angel.

True Believers

A few years ago, a revealing tragicomedy took place in Venezuela's plains region. The drama began when a handful of campesinos in the state of Barinas responded enthusiastically to Chávez's call to make communes. These were the truest of Chavista true believers. They set up their own commune and called it Eje Socialista (Socialist Axis). Ingenuous to the core, the Eje Socialista communards decided to completely disobey the state. For them, the commune was the new authority, and the only one. They believed this totally and stuck to it until the end. After all, Chávez, though dead, was on their side! These forthright communards were bold and honest. Nevertheless, after a few clashes with state authorities, all of them wound up in prison.

The communards at El Maizal are not as extreme as those of Eje Socialista, nor as ingenuous. Yet, their dance with state authorities involves some of the same moves. It is true that they make a cult out of Chávez—who is painted, sculpted, and inscribed all over their commune—but, like most cults, El Maizal's way of paying homage to the dead leader can be highly subversive. It is always heretical to communicate directly with the maximum authority, without any mediation of high priests. Moreover, for El Maizal's communards, loyalty to the former president also implies that they do not have to obey anyone else! So, the commune carries out its interpretation of Chávez's legacy, and that can mean anything from disregarding private property to defying government officials.

We are assembled in a thatched-roof *caney*, not far from El Maizal's stern-looking bronze bust of Chávez, who seems to keep vigil over our meeting. Communard Jenifer Lamus is with us explaining her work as an organizer of corn and cattle production. She is a good example of this commune's radical independence in the name of authority. "For my part," Lamus states, "I always say that El Maizal got where it is because of the rebelliousness of the army of women and men who make this whole project possible."

It is working people who are at the center of this communal farm. They make the decisions but do so with a mandate that is beyond question. "When Chávez said, 'Commune or Nothing!' that order was carried out here, and it became our horizon. And we always say that we are willing to give up our lives for it. . . . If there is an obstacle, then we'll overcome it. Nothing should stand in the way of Chávez's dream."

Now the meaning of the grim face on El Maizal's Chávez bust is becoming clearer to me (I am warming up to it!). These people are seriously unwilling to back down before capitalist roaders in the government or among their land-owning neighbors. Lamus points out how the government hindering access to basic farm inputs can impede the commune's development, as happened two years ago, when El Maizal was facing the prospect of having no corn crop that season because the state institution AgroPatria refused to sell them seeds. Desperate, Prado and others decided to get the seeds by hook or by crook and bought them on the black market. The police soon arrived to put him and a few of his fellows in jail. Even so, the commune was undaunted. Had not Chávez himself spent a great deal of time behind bars? A flurry of phone calls later to sympathetic lawyers and Chavista politicians in Caracas and they were all set free.

To overcome problems such as this, El Maizal is trying to join forces with other communes around the country. With this in mind, they have recently taken the lead in launching the Communard Union, an association of communes on a national level, which works to link up and strengthen those organizations committed to communal socialism in the country (discussed in chapter 6). The participating communes are already exchanging work brigades and supplying products to each other outside of the capitalist market. Lamus explains: "We are convinced that Chávez's idea does not have to be a dream. . . . The Communard Union shows that many more people are joining forces with the communal project. That is how we can advance with this marvelous idea."

Despite their occasional clashes with the government, everyone at El Maizal has internalized a keen political sense that keeps them from romanticizing the commune's autonomy or from thinking of the Venezuelan state in unidimensional terms. These are lessons learned from Chavismo's trajectory over the past two decades. This experience showed that popular power—grassroots control over the political and economic dimensions of a community—can grow much more solidly if it exists in a dialectical relation with the state. State support for autonomous projects might be anything from material assistance to a legal framework that defends popular power. The upshot of twenty years of Chavista experimentation, registered in the minds of millions of Venezuelans, is that state institutions, when sympathetic, can allow popular power to flourish locally and even project itself nationally and internationally.

The communal movement's complex way of relating to the state is part of Venezuela's special history, which includes its key role in founding the Organization of the Petroleum Exporting Countries. Over the last one hundred years, people here have internalized the idea that the country's oil and mineral resources belong to them collectively and should be used for popular welfare and grassroots development. They reason: the economic muscle of the state might not always be in the service of the common people, but it should be! Perhaps a fitting picture of this dialectical relation, this push and pull between sometimes sympathetic state institutions and defiant grassroots independence, is the image of this young communard seated near the figure of Chávez. She is appealing to the bronze president's authority but doing so to defy the state in the name of a higher power!

A TIME CAPSULE

Sometimes an idea can bounce around in history before it finds a place where it can really take root. Chavismo first emerged among Venezuela's urban masses and then, as is well known, broke into state circles and even came to hegemonize the region's geopolitics. Soon, however, Chavismo began to be rolled back. It had a hard time weathering the economic crisis of 2008 and the falling oil prices that came later. A carefully executed coup d'état in Honduras—hitting at what was clearly the weak link in the chain of emancipated countries—was one of the first imperialist victories against Chavista internationalism. Bureaucratization, stagnation, the leader's poor health, and finally his death came next. Problems with succession and infighting were almost inevitable.

To many, it looked like Chavismo might completely disappear along with its leader, or that it would be deformed unrecognizably by the sanctions. Yet, all that was on the surface, far from the invisible movements of history that are often the most important ones. A not so well-known (but crucially important) development was that this mostly urban revolutionary movement had also made deep inroads into the rural regions. There, ordinary people, who were somewhat removed from the vicissitudes of official politics and the global economy, had also heard Chávez's discourse, and they hearkened especially to his call to organize themselves and build communes. That is to say, Chavismo had quietly taken root in places that were not so visible: in the interstices of Venezuelan society and particularly in rural redoubts.

The biography of Prado, El Maizal's main spokesperson, reflects the tortuous urban-rural trajectory of Chavista ideology. When young, Prado had been a coffee farmer in the area. However, he sold his farm and went to the city, becoming involved in politics. Along with thousands of other Venezuelan youths, Prado traveled to Cuba as part of the Frente Francisco de Miranda and, after returning, militated in that Chavista youth organization. Still, this lasted only until his support for a Communist Party candidate in regional elections got him expelled. Cast outside of the political sphere, Prado went back to his hometown, but without land, he ended up having to work security on a local farm complex. This farm later became El Maizal Commune. When a local group started to make moves to occupy the land he was guarding, Prado told his boss not to count on him and joined their ranks.

Prado's life has been marked by many such odd twists and turns, most of them very fortunate. In 2009, he was lucky enough to be in the audience of the historic television program *Aló Presidente Teórico No. 1* when Chávez laid out the theoretical basis of the commune, explaining the role of social property (while joking that many had interpreted socialism as a mere verbal baptism).[1] From the crowd, Prado spoke up and told Chávez about the land they had just occupied in Simón Planas township and their plans to manage it collectively. That year, Chávez visited El Maizal twice, leaving a permanent mark on the community and seeming to presage its extraordinary future.

Now, Prado is seated in the commune's tiny office telling us how Chávez's thinking about productive relations developed along with the practical experience of the Venezuelan masses: "Chávez's theory evolved over time. He began with the cooperatives, but then realized that cooperatives only maintained the logic of private property. So, Chávez began to seek a form based on *social property*, and that is how the commune came about." Prado's assertion that cooperatives repeat the logic of private property might sound surprising. But these are lessons the Chavista movement learned both through its own concrete experience and by studying Yugoslavia's socialist history. As these past experiences show, a cooperatively run enterprise can have many owners—even completely equal ones—but still not serve the whole society, as should be the aim of social property.

El Maizal takes these lessons to heart. To comply with the social property model, the commune is not only democratically run (it has an internal parliament that decides what it will produce and how), but it is also very careful about what happens with its surpluses. In explaining the difference between cooperative private property and social property, Prado offers us an example: "If El Maizal were simply a cooperative, the surplus would go back into the production units here or it would be distributed among the co-op's members. But that is not the case. Instead, because El Maizal is a commune, we redistribute the surplus through various social channels, and it can even be used to promote production in other communes."

Prado is always thinking about how to spread the communal model, since improving the whole society's well-being is the movement's strategic goal. He and his colleagues reach out to other communities to pursue this aim, offering them both moral and material support. Just now, Prado is bubbling with enthusiasm about a newly founded commune in one of the poorest neighborhoods nearby. That community is mostly made up of women and children living in mud-hut *ranchos*. Respiratory problems are common among the group, which has also been hit hard by COVID. When the women started the commune, their main project was to acquire a *nebulización* (asthma treatment) center for their neighborhood, which they did by putting posters of Chávez and Che Guevara on a small hut and insisting that the state provide the medical equipment. They christened their project *Negra Hipólita*, after Simón Bolívar's wet nurse.

Prado is passionate about this new initiative. It seems to prove his point that ordinary people, by organizing, can advance their goals even in a context of crisis, sanctions, and widespread political backpedaling. He believes that one can expand the grassroots basis of socialism—democratic control of resources—despite many external threats and high levels of internal defeatism. "The commune is a struggle of the *pueblo*. And the *pueblo* doesn't just produce, participate, and defend the project. We also aspire to have popular control and self-government in the whole territory. . . . The Chavista struggle for justice in these rural areas won't stop."

CONFLICT AND RESISTANCE

Over the past two decades, the government's agrarian policy

has tended to swing between voluntarism and pragmatism. The mainstays of the Bolivarian Process may have been essentially urban and military, but the government still had to determine what its rural policy would be. The 2001 Land Law, which allowed for the occupation of unused land, was indeed very radical, and in fact became a precipitating factor for the 2002 coup d'état. Likewise, Chávez's longstanding agricultural minister Elías Jaua and successor Juan Carlos Loyo were both generally left leaning, a high point in their tenures being the sweeping land expropriations of 2006–2009. Unfortunately, many of the ministry's more radical projects at the time failed to connect with social movements in the rural areas, and ministry officials were willing to hypocritically inaugurate projects that barely existed.

In 2009 and 2010, Chávez began to promote the commune, which was clearly a revolutionary option for rural Venezuela. Yet, after Chávez died and Maduro took over, the fledgling agriculture minister Yván Gil adopted a more pragmatic approach, including pacts with the rural bourgeoisie, the so-called "producers." When current agricultural minister Wilmar Castro Soteldo came on the scene a few years later, that pragmatism became outright class collaboration, with the rural bourgeoisie being declared "revolutionary." In a surprising move, Castro Soteldo went on television and delivered long, eclectic discourses—even quoting Sor Juana Inés de la Cruz, the Mexican poet-nun- -to explain how Venezuela's bourgeoisie could be revolutionary. At least you could not blame the minister for playing his cards too close to his chest!

The communards at El Maizal oppose Castro Soteldo's capitalist-roader tendency, which they call reformism. (Perhaps more than *reformist*, the minister should be called *antipopular*. As Prado says: "If you really want to change things, you have to give power over to the people," which Castro Soteldo seems unwilling to do.) To combat this kind of institutional backsliding and leverage the government, El Maizal's communards are employing a number of tactics in what they see as a battle to force President

Maduro and his cabinet over to their side. Part of this struggle is a huge drive for political education of people in the region, to raise levels of ideological formation. Another part of their plan is the Communard Union: reaching out to other communes and preaching by the example of solidarity. Finally, and much more controversially, they have a newly hatched project to make Prado into the local mayor. By obtaining the post, the commune's main spokesperson is supposed to achieve practical solutions for the community (solving their garbage disposal and seed problems, for example) and also speak up for socialism inside the government apparatus.

Some of the commune's most trusted sympathizers are skeptical about this latest move. Will an official position distract Prado from grassroots work? Could holding power in the township's government corrupt El Maizal's leaders? Whatever one's doubts about this new effort—and I share them—it is impressive to see the campaign the commune is carrying out in the week of our visit. Elections involving massive mobilization are a Venezuelan specialty. It is a terrain they navigate with great skill—evidence of the unique Chavista experience of repurposing elections for revolutionary ends. During the course of the summer, the tasks of going house to house, and of rallying people with enthusiasm and "mystique" have consumed many of the commune's militants. The social networks that El Maizal employs have also become torrents of information related to the campaign, along with images of marches, neighborhood cookouts, and other gatherings.[2]

Inadvertently, I make a contribution to Prado's campaign imagery. It happens because I was invited to join El Maizal's WhatsApp group and many of the group's users reached out to me with hearty welcomes. Not knowing how to respond, being out of my element in social networks, I sent a smiley face and then hunted down the red flag emoticon to accompany it. The little red flag turned out to be a huge hit in the midst of the election campaign. El Maizal's communards began to tag most of the photos of marches, rallies, and meetings related to the campaign with one or more waving flags (often coupled with flexed biceps and raised fists).

Why was the red flag icon so popular at El Maizal? It might be because Chávez had used "socialist red" in his campaigns, whereas the current government's commitment to that project (and color!) seems to be more precarious. Alternatively, it could be simply that socialist references reach deeply into Venezuela's history, having been lodged there by the communist-affiliated movements that rose up and dominated the country's left from the 1960s through the 1980s. Whichever of these motives is most relevant, I am delighted by the headway made by the red flag in this commune because it points to the persistence of very "red" elements in the so-called Pink Tide. However, it also raises the question of the role of the past and historical memory in shaping the communes, which is the subject of our next chapter.

2

The Long Roots of Venezuela's Communal Tradition

S ocialist communes may be new in Venezuela—officially, they began no earlier than 2009—but, like much that is new, they also rely on old traditions and thus connect with past social formations. On a certain level, it is hardly surprising that overcoming the radical atomization and isolated individuality of capitalist society could be inspired by elements of past social formations inasmuch as these latter, especially those dating from prehistory, were overwhelmingly communitarian. However, much of the Marxist left has fallen into the trap of thinking that a socialist future will be generated, if not *ex nihilo*, at least without much reference to past epochs and their social forms. In defense of this latter approach, one can appeal to Marx himself, who wrote that bourgeois revolutions appeal to history ("to smother their own content") but proletarian revolutions take their poetry from the future.[1] This statement is no outlier. In fact, the young Marx generally assumed that capitalism would simply erase and overcome earlier forms of domination. This overly sanguine, essentially progressive view of capitalism surely played a role in the young Marx's taking distance from such earlier social formations. He looked to them mostly for what they might reveal to the investigator when juxtaposed to capitalism, but he thought of them very little in terms of models.[2] As we shall see, Marx later revised this idea, coming to embrace the relevance of communitarian traditions, past and present, for the socialist future, and he began to see pre-capitalist social formations as genuine assets in socialist construction.

However, this shift in Marx's thought in relation to pre-capitalist societies is not well known, and it has not kept most Marxists and the bulk of the socialist movement from radically downplaying the importance of our various communitarian histories. Latin America may be an exception to this general theoretical trend, for the simple reason that the continent's past weighs so heavily on its present. This is in part because of the radical expressions of uneven and combined development that occur in such dependent countries, which allow pre-capitalist formations to survive and thus encourage many political movements to appeal to them. In Venezuela, some academics and revolutionaries have argued for the pertinence of the region's communal past—and the communitarian practices that survive there today—to the project of socialist construction. Among the most distinguished of these theorists are anthropologists Iraida Vargas and Mario Sanoja, who have claimed that both Venezuela's history and its longstanding cultural traditions could be the basis of the Bolivarian Process's development of communal socialism. For this reason, it is important to consider the profound links that this pair of researchers has uncovered between the future that the Bolivarian Revolution aspires to and its roots in a society whose practices of solidarity and deep-seated conceptions of equality are often shaped by Indigenous and African traditions. Their arguments, sketched below, coincide both with the multilinear approach to historical development that Marx finally espoused and with some subaltern theoretical Marxian currents in Latin America.

INCAN COMMUNISM

In Latin American Marxist theory, the first great—and still the most famous—"blast from the past" came from Peruvian Marxist José Carlos Mariátegui. In 1928, he published his watershed work, *7 Interpretive Essays on Peruvian Reality*.[3] This work went against the grain of socialist thought at the time. While most of Marxism was riding high on the workers' victory in the incipient USSR and had its gaze directed toward the *final struggle* that would usher in the glorious communist future, Mariátegui cast his vision toward the past of his Andean country. His creative approach to Marxism sent shockwaves through the consensus of the Third International, which in a Eurocentric way had determined that Latin America's "semi-feudal" societies had nothing to offer the socialist project. For his part, Mariátegui was, in his own words, a "convinced and confessed" Marxist. However, he was unable to accept the Third International's rote rejection of Latin America's past. Instead, he argued that the collective nature of Incan society, especially the lack of private property in land, represented a "communist past" in the Andean region that, far from being dead, constituted a living legacy that could inspire present and future post-capitalist constructions.

Mariátegui's essay, "The Problem of the Land," which appears third in the *7 Essays* collection, presents this claim clearly. There he wrote that liberal-style land reform in Peru, which some called for at the time, was not the solution for overcoming the *latifundio* and Indigenous servitude in his country. He thought that the historical moment to divide the land into small parcels had passed. Instead, an overtly socialist and collective solution was possible and even necessary, because of the "undeniable and concrete factor which gives its peculiar character to our agrarian problem: the survival of the community and of elements of a practical socialism in Indigenous agriculture and life."[4] Mariátegui's idea—and by "community" he was referring to Indigenous *ayllus*[5]—was that there was enough alive of what he called "Incan communism" to pursue a collective approach to land reform. In effect, the pre-colonial past and its forms of land tenure could be reactivated in the present to construct a socialist future.

This claim of Mariátegui flew in the face of Eurocentric Marxist currents, whose proponents saw Incan civilization as merely a local variant of feudalism. Yet Mariátegui's approach did resonate with a widespread cultural tendency that existed in Europe and elsewhere: Romanticism. In Michael Löwy's words, Romanticism is essentially "a cultural protest against modern capitalist civilization based on social, cultural, political or religious values [that] are precapitalist or premodern or preindustrial."[6] This kind of romanticism is widespread in Latin America, where the ghosts of the past (Simón Bolívar, José Martí, Emiliano Zapata, Guacaipuro) often seem more alive than the wan politics of the living. Revolutionaries often invoke these fig-ures in struggles against capitalism and imperialism in the region. However, in Mariátegui's case, a commitment to historical mate-rialism—a result of his embracing of Marxism while living in Italy in the 1920s—gave his approach to the continent's past a more robust and scientific character. Hence, with one eye on the past and another on the present, Mariátegui understood communism to be not only an existential issue of the continent—"only a social-ist Latin America could stand up to a capitalist North America," he wrote—but he also saw it as one that had connections reach-ing far into its past.[7]

THE LAST MARX AND THE RUSSIAN COMMUNE

Mariátegui's unorthodox views led to heated debates with the more dogmatic theorists in the Third International, who con-tended that Latin America's underdeveloped countries, mired in feudal forms, could only aspire to a stage of capitalist devel-opment in the short and even middle term. These theorists invoked "Marx" to defend this doctrinaire, "stagist" position. Still, unbeknownst to them, Mariátegui's thinking resonated with the direction taken by Marx's mature thought—especially the work of the so-called Last Marx—on the issue of the relevance of communitarian life-forms to socialism. This is a part of Marx's life and production that has only come to light recently, thanks to studies such as those of Teodor Shanin, Kevin Anderson, and Marcello Musto.[8] What we know now is that after publishing *Capital,* volume 1, in 1867, Marx continued to investigate insatiably, casting his attention toward the periphery of capitalism and also assimilating the findings brought by social science's recent discovery of prehistory. The new field of prehistory, which revealed that humanoids had lived on the earth for millions of years, had an enormous impact on how human life and human development were viewed at the time—not the least because it opened a window on what came to be called "primitive communism." Marx also began to study Russia in detail in the 1870s, even learning the language. He had a particular interest in Russian forms of land tenure, including the survival of the peasant commune in that country, and he began communicating with Russian intellectuals and militants.

One of these was the former populist Vera Zasulich. Zasulich had become famous for attempting to assassinate a tsarist official, before co-founding the Marxist "Emancipation of Labor" group with Georgi Plekhanov. She wrote to Marx in 1881 about the controversial issue of the Russian peasant commune (the *obshchina*), asking whether it could be an asset in constructing socialism, as some Russian populists argued, or whether it would simply have to disappear, making way for a long stage of capitalist development. Zasulich might have thought that, given Marx's earlier defense of progressive development through capitalism (even when brought about by colonialists!), he would acknowledge the need for the peasant commune to disappear. Yet Marx's thinking, perhaps under the influence of the Paris Commune (1871), was now going in a different direction. His historiography had taken a distinctively Romantic turn from the mid-1850s forward. For Marx now, pre-capitalist social formations were no longer seen

as simply dead and irretrievable, and the egalitarian and more
sustainable relations in many Indigenous societies interested him
greatly.[9] Human development, instead of being linear and progressive, was in this new view more like a curved circuit in which
the communal forms embodied in precapitalist social formations
could potentially touch off and ignite the future.

In this spirit, in composing his various drafts to Zasulich,
Marx came to affirm that Russia's old-fashioned peasant communes were not necessarily doomed to disappear but could
instead be a "fulcrum of social regeneration" and a "direct starting point of the system to which contemporary society strives."[10]
Backtracking on what he had claimed earlier in *Capital* 1—that
"the more industrially developed country only shows, to the less
developed, the image of its own future"—Marx was now suggest-
ing that "less-developed" societies might hold a few lessons of
their own for the future, particularly regarding their communal
forms. Importantly, he pointed out that the historical sequence
of modes of production he had discussed in *Capital* and elsewhere was confined to "the countries of Western Europe" and he
believed in no one-size-fits-all "historico-philosophical theory."
Marx's letter and drafts to Zasulich were lost and would only
be discovered in 1911. It was David Riazanov, the outstanding
director of the Marx-Engels Institute, who found them. Yet the
letters remained unpublished until 1924. Not surprisingly, in a
Soviet Union where a modernizing, stagist Marx was becoming
something of a religion, this alternative and "Romantic" vision of
Marx generated little enthusiasm.

CARIBBEAN ANARCHISM

Despite having little access to the writings of the Last Marx,
Marxists in Latin America were forced early on to reckon with
the revolutionary potential of their own communitarian traditions, and also with the emancipatory aspects of historical
memory. Theorists in the region were embedded in situations

that were amenable to this line of thought, inasmuch as wherever capitalism is an outside imposition, popular culture tends to defend regional tradition in the face of foreign aggressors. Whatever the reasons, this past-oriented, Romantic vision is widespread in the continent's Marxism. It existed in Peru, as we have seen with Mariátegui's work, and it also had expressions in Cuba, where the philosopher and historian Fernando Martínez Heredia argued that the Cuban Revolution of 1959 had deep roots in nineteenth- and early twentieth-century movements for emancipation. Similar claims are also being made in Venezuela today. Venezuela's pre-colonial past is less known and less studied than the Andean civilization of the Incas or that of the Aztecs in what is today Mexico. Nevertheless, the decentralized and horizontally structured Indigenous societies that existed—and in important cases, still exist—in much of Venezuela's territory deserve careful attention, because they provide potential bases for a socialist future, and especially for the communal construction of a post-capitalist society.

This is the most important argument of the Venezuelan anthropologists Iraida Vargas and Mario Sanoja. It grows organically out of their earlier research. Sanoja, who died in 2022, was best known for his investigations into agrarian practices in what he called the "north of South America." That research is summarized in a small book titled *Los hombres de la yuca y el maíz* (1977), which highlights the importance of *vegeculture*, the cultivation of roots rather than grains, in shaping pre-colonial Indigenous communities in much of what is today Venezuela. To write this epoch-making book, Sanoja had to cast off the yoke of what could be facetiously called "Mexican cultural hegemony," as expressed in the idea that Latin Americans are essentially *people of corn*. The problem with that idea is that it underplays the critical role of vegeculture, not only of potatoes in the Andes but of yuca in what is much of Venezuela and Brazil. Yuca is a crop that requires relatively little attention, allows for long-term storage in the ground, and, in its bitter form, is highly imperishable. Its cultivation went hand in hand with a specific kind of social formation: communities that were decentralized and mostly horizontal, with only temporary leaderships. Sanoja called these formations "autarkic and politically independent"—in short, they were anarchist![11]

For anyone who has lived some time in Venezuela, it is easy to believe the formative influence of this Indigenous inheritance—characterized by horizontality and independence—on the country and its cultures. On the one hand, there are the egalitarian social practices that operate in the communities of Warao, Yukpa, Wayuu, Kariña, Yanomami, Pemon, and other Indigenous peoples that maintain their cultural identity and regional autonomy. On the other hand, the effects of such traditions and values extend widely into the society, even permeating urban popular culture. One surprising expression of this legacy is seen in Venezuelans' complex attitude toward their leaders, Hugo Chávez included, to whom they pay allegiance to carry out specific tasks but at the same time treat with gratifying familiarity most of the time (as just one person among many in the collective). Then there are the collective egalitarian labor practices, *cayapas*, that are assumed with great enthusiasm and can be intense, lasting for days, along with the widespread practice of organizing collective soup meals, called *sancochos*.[12] All this is to say that Vargas and Sanoja, in their various works that defend the importance of Venezuelan traditions in building a new communal world, were theorizing based on what one can see before one's eyes in the country and in its diverse cultures.

A Very Long Revolution

Though their intellectual trajectory dates back well into the twentieth century, Vargas and Sanoja both became enthusiastic Chavistas. Hence, when the late Hugo Chávez proposed the communal path to socialism in 2009, they began to scour the country's prehistoric and historic past for precedents to the project of communal socialism. The anthropologist couple is profoundly influenced by historians of the French *Annales* school, who gave importance to the sociological dimensions of history and employed the perspective of the *longue durée*. This intellectual training prepared them to chart the relevance of Venezuela's communal traditions, as they survive in specific locations and in everyday culture, to the work of building the socialist, communal future. With a nod to Maoism, they titled their resulting work, *La larga marcha hacia la sociedad communal* (2017). The book has two main themes. On the one hand, it looks at how the "hidden nation," made up of impoverished, racialized masses, has pushed forward an emancipatory project for more than two centuries (issuing into the Bolivarian Revolution today). On the other hand, it addresses how Venezuela's current socialist project can be based on communitarian traditions derived from diverse practices and attitudes still persisting in the society.

This may seem an excessively general argument, but it translates into some specific, concrete claims about regions and projects in Venezuela. For example, the authors point out how in central-western Lara State, where some of Venezuela's most important communes exist today, there was once a huge Indigenous civilization that had developed proto-state structures and wide-ranging territorial control. These were the Caquetío people, and part of their legacy consists of deep-rooted communitarian traditions, including a vast system of cooperatives of weavers and pottery makers that exchanged their goods in the zone.[13] For Sanoja and Vargas, it is easy to draw a line from that past civilization to the communal present in the region, where strong community organizations such as Cecosesola, Plan Pueblo a Pueblo, and El Maizal figure prominently. If this appears to be a radical form of historical telescoping, the argument is nevertheless backed up by the existence of enduring production practices, aimed at satisfying society's necessities, which the researcher pair calls the "true social cement that in the last instance supports the revolutionary or counterrevolutionary imaginary of social collectives."

Another concrete example of how their argument plays out is found in the 23 de Enero barrio of Caracas, where powerful organizations such as La Piedrita, Alexis Vive (El Panal Commune), and Coordinadora Simón Bolívar, are flourishing. Vargas and Sanoja argue that the communitarian traditions that operate in that barrio are derived from the largely Afro-Venezuelan populations that settled there some seventy years ago. Such communities draw from the long tradition of Maroon resistance and practices of self-governance developed by Venezuelan Afro-descended people in their longstanding efforts to maintain cultural identity, freedom, and egalitarian social relations, in the face of enduring discrimination and exclusion. The communities in 23 de Enero are close-knit, without the atomization found in many urban centers around the world. For example, the Catholic religious festivals there show diverse African influences, while functioning to maintain community cohesion and sometimes even promote revolutionary ideology. Security is also under community control: in many sectors of the barrio, the police do not enter, but order is maintained by community organizations. In recent decades, confirming Vargas and Sanoja's general thesis, one can see how even the social peace maintained by the barrio's grassroots *colectivos* (self-organized urban groups) has begun to take on a socialist character, with their leaders assuming revolutionary positions (see chapter 8).

HISTORY FROM BELOW

Another theoretical influence on the anthropologist couple is English Marxist historian E. P. Thompson, who figures in their bibliographies along with Marc Bloch and Fernand Braudel of the *Annales* school. That is because Vargas and Sanoja's work connects with Thompson's thesis that the working masses are not a passive product of the capitalist productive apparatus, which spits out a generic bourgeoisie on one end and a generic proletariat on the other, but rather these masses produce themselves as a class, projecting futures and even new forms of societal organization. Generic or abstract working classes, which exist only on paper, may seem short on ideas for how to construct the future. However, *actually existing* working classes, in Venezuela and elsewhere, are steeped in historical memory and usually aspire to civilizational projects that are cobbled together from elements of the known—that is, from old social forms and collective memory—but even so contain an emancipatory dimension because the values they express were developed over time as part of the culture of the oppressed.

In the Venezuelan case, there is a 500-year-old history of resistance to class and (neo)colonial oppression. Rebellions of diverse kinds took place long before the independence wars against the Spanish metropolis set off an ongoing class struggle that persists up to the present. This much is well-traveled territory and investigated by many anthropologists and historians. However, what Vargas and Sanoja wish to highlight in relation to future socialist constructions, is that these earlier rebellions were not merely spontaneous actions but rather rich in programmatic content, projecting alternative forms of government and society. For example, some of the revolts of enslaved people aspired to create kingdoms that had a decidedly utopian dimension, envisioning multicultural coexistence with creole settlers, whereas others, such as the heroic rebellion led by José Leonardo Chirino in Coro, were likely inspired by the emancipatory project of the Haitian Revolution as well as by communal traditions from West and Central Africa.[14] Also of great relevance were the nineteenth-century mass movements, most notably the one led by Ezequiel Zamora, that took the European idea of federalism and in a paradoxical way filled it with an anti-oligarchical content. Insofar as these diverse historical struggles continue to shape Venezuelan society, Vargas and Sanoja are able to bring a novel perspective to the circles of Chavista intellectuality. Their view, inspired by the tradition of popular historiography, is that the Bolivarian Revolution, and its current commune-based strategy, is the culmination of a series of struggles and aspirations reaching back at least half a millennium in the region.

The Historical Current

This thesis about the relevance of the past to contemporary socialism in Venezuela receives support from the most diverse quarters. An important, if surprising one, comes from the experience of the Venezuelan guerrilla. This armed movement was born in the early 1960s as the Venezuelan Communist Party fell under extreme persecution. Its militants, despite the university contexts from which most were drawn, came to know the rural communities and their belief systems well during their almost two decades of clandestine struggle. After their military defeat in the late 1970s, the Venezuelan guerrilla changed methods of struggle for more long-term, community-based ones. At about the same time, they began to refer to the continuity of struggles that reached from deep in Venezuelan history to the present as the "historical current." Their claim was inspired by what they had seen firsthand. For example, in one of the mountainous regions where the guerrilla melded best with the communities and lasted longest, there is a legacy of enduring Indigenous and Maroon resistance. This territory includes the mountains of Yaracuy and Lara, where Miguel de Buría led a rebellion of enslaved people beginning in the mid-sixteenth century, forming common cause with the Jirajara nation that the Spanish could not dominate. Their struggle lasted more than seventy-five years, with Indigenous and Afro-descended people together consolidating a large liberated area, a self-governed Maroon community, which Venezuelans call a "*cumbe*." Eventually, the Spanish throne, outfought and outwitted, had no choice but to recognize this territory as an independent political entity.[15] The memory of this anti-colonial struggle persists in local legends, the best known of which figures the partner of Miguel de Buría as Maria Lionza, an Indigenous chieftess who rides a tapir.

This Maroon community would go on holding the land in common and having its own internal governance. However, they had a serious setback when a nineteenth-century judge, Fernando Espinal, declared the inhabitants to be mere *"campesinos"* or peasants, thus ending their legal status as an Indigenous reserve.[16] This opened the doors to private ownership. In higher altitude zones, which were suitable for coffee growing, the Giménez family entered, holding much of the land during the late nineteenth century and the first half of the twentieth century. The towns in that zone still bear the names of their coffee plantations: Buenos Aires, Copei, etc. Somewhat later, large swaths of the lower-lying lands came under control of Cuban sugar planters, who had been displaced by the 1959 revolution. In both places, the original inhabitants were reduced to day laborers who worked on the plantations of the oligarchical landlords. Yet the tradition of resistance and the memory of the struggle continued. For example, at one point in the mid-1980s, a group of politically conscious student activists joined forces with farmworkers to occupy a large tract of land in the Los Cañizos Palo Quemao hacienda, while the Bolivarian Revolution with its 2001 Land Law gave further impetus to efforts to recover the land, opening the door for more grassroots land occupations—often by the very descendants of those who had lived in the earlier Maroon community—and more liberated territory. This allowed for the formation of cooperatives, which benefited from state-supplied farm machinery, and it later opened the way for the construction of socialist communes, such as the Alí Primera and Hugo Chávez communes now thriving in Urachiche.[17]

The historical line that reaches more or less without break from the region liberated by Miguel de Buría's followers and their Jirajara allies—among the hundreds of self-governed *cumbes* that were once sown across the Venezuelan territory, forming powerful interethnic resistance systems—to Bolivarian cooperatives and communes today is the best proof for the existence of a "historical current."[18] However, the evidence that past struggles are a living and charged legacy is obvious to any visitor to Yaracuy today. That is because when approaching Yaracuy's capital city San Felipe, one encounters numerous outsized statues of saints and virgins that line the roadway, like concrete sentinels. This itself is present-day evidence of the struggle, for these statues are part of the ideological campaign against Indigenous resistance. The other side of the coin—the symbols of rebellion that form the counterpoint to these Christian icons—are the syncretic altars that exist in the nearby mountains rendering homage to María Lionza, Miguel de Buría, Simón Bolívar, and now Hugo Chávez. Just as Afro-descendant and Indigenous people fought together for centuries to maintain or recover their land from the onslaught of colonists and oligarchical landlords, so the spiritual avatars of each side go on being deployed to win over hearts and minds for one camp or the other in this ongoing class war.

THE ONCE AND FUTURE COMMUNE

The truth is that any given society, far from being a tabula rasa, is a rich palimpsest made up of many elements from the living past. This is what Vargas and Sanoja, on the one hand, and the Venezuelan guerrilla, on the other, discovered. Chávez himself was aware of this fact. In *Aló Presidente Teórico No. 1*, where Chávez opened a whole new epoch of socialist construction with his assertion that the commune is "the space in which socialism will be born," he also referred to the importance of Indigenous societies both in Venezuela and in the South American continent more generally to building socialist communes in contemporary times.[19] To this effect, he brandished and quoted from a book he had read in his youth about the socialism of the Incas: Louis Baudin's *El imperio socialista de los Incas*. The key point is that the spaces of Venezuelan society should not be seen in abstract terms, but instead as concrete and varied formations that are traversed by diverse cultural codes and longstanding patterns of behavior. As far as socialist construction is concerned, the most important features in this sense are that—along with the surviving Indigenous communities which already embody many socialist values —the country's social fabric contains practices of communitarian coexistence, varied forms of social solidarity, and above all many surviving expressions of egalitarian social relations.

This living legacy has a relevance that goes beyond the microlevel of the isolated *cumbe* or community, for the Indigenous and Afro-Venezuelan inheritance includes the possibility of reactivating an alternative "geometry of power," based on pre-colonial and Maroon networks that once existed throughout the territory, which could be revived and adapted in the process of building socialism. Both the civilization of the Caquetío, who had a network reaching out into the Caribbean islands, and the collaboration between Indigenous and Afro-descendant Maroon communities in resistance, provide potential models for a future confederation of self-organized communities. This possibility jibes with the vision endorsed by most supporters of Venezuela's communal movement, who believe that the socialist future in Venezuela should be based on a network of communal organizations that cooperatively produce to satisfy their own collective needs, and share their surpluses with other organized communities, through a widening web of non-market relations based on solidarity. Such a vision is not strictly anti-statist, but rather posits the Venezuelan state as initially coexisting in a dialectical relation with a plurality of self-organized communes. Later, as the transition process advances, the state will be transcended and surpassed by the forces of communal organization. It is surely a positive sign that this grassroots vision of social transformation coincides with Marx's overall conceptualization of communist society as consisting of communities of "freely associated producers" and is underpinned by the German theorist's mature theoretical analyses. The latter locate social domination in the whole gamut of capitalism's historically specific categories, which implies that emancipation requires abolishing not just the exploitation of workers (as the hegemonic communist movements maintained throughout the twentieth

century) but also the commodity form, wages, and alienated, proletarian labor in general.

In the foregoing, following Marx and other theorists, we have
argued that past social or living communitarian formations can
help us to develop integral solutions to building the new society
that overcomes the totality of capitalism's alienating categories.
Importantly, however, this perspective on the past requires that
we revise our approach to what in Marxism is usually known
as "primitive" or "original accumulation." Those terms, which
partly refer to the processes of destruction and expropriation of
original communities on the way to building capitalism, must
be approached differently. *Progressivist* or *modernizing* currents
of Marxism have tended to see primitive accumulation, or the
separation of direct producers from their labor conditions, as
just an inevitable, if very painful, step toward explaining capitalist
exploitation and surplus value extraction. However, this process
of expropriation should be considered more carefully, in ways
that go beyond the progressivist, stagist narrative. In fact, Marx's
ongoing work on both past and living Indigenous communities,
begun in the *Grundrisse* but continuing through to the end of his
life, are evidence that ultimately he adopted a more respectful,
inquisitive, and affirmative perspective on the original communities that often fall victim to processes of capitalist expropriation.
The key issue is that the wounds opened by primitive accumulation, through processes that continue in the present, are far from
over and done with, as some have insinuated. For those committed to healing those wounds (overcoming that separation) under
a new modality, current research into the separation of producers from their labor conditions should address both the larger
question of the alienation that this step produces—how it spells
loss of control, loss of meaning and dignity, along with, of course,
laying the ground for exploitation—and also examine the possibilities, implicit in *revolutionary Romantic* approaches, for
maintaining or restoring the integrity of pre-capitalist formations
in new, modern conditions.[20]

Universal Lessons?

Romantic or "back-to-the-future" theses about socialist construction—and this holds true whether they are advanced by Marx, Mariátegui, Vargas and Sanoja, Chávez, or the Venezuelan guerrilla—always raise questions related to their specificity and hence their range of application. Are these ideas relevant to other parts of the world, not just Venezuela, Peru, and elsewhere in Latin America? As we have argued, in line with this general perspective, the building of the socialist commune in Venezuela should be greatly facilitated by both the existing Indigenous communities and the persistence of aspects of a generalized communal inheritance both in Venezuela's rural and urban cultures. Such an approach is quite convincing in a country characterized in the extreme by "uneven and combined development" and in a cultural context where historical memory figures extensively in both the quotidian imagination and political discourse. But what about the rest of the world, including regions that might be lacking in these particularities? The relevance of communal traditions for other regions of the world is a question that can only be resolved through a close examination that considers their past and present cultural specificities.

In effect, the thesis leaves open the question of how socialist construction should proceed in regions poorer in community traditions, with weaker connections to the "practical socialism" embodied in many pre-capitalist social formations. What will their way of overcoming the totality of capitalist relations look like? Another way of phrasing the same question is: How much of the socialist commune, as it is conceived in Venezuela today, is particular to that concrete situation, and how much of it is relevant to the universal project of socialist construction?[21] Though the relation between the general and the particular in the Venezuelan case may be difficult to hash out, a preliminary answer is that some form of community production is surely needed for socialist construction—communities are, after all, where directly social labor takes place, if that means labor that is not mediated by the market but by conscious and collective decision-making. Hence, the general claim is the need to have freely associated producers abolish the commodity form and the entire gamut of social relations that derive from it. However, the exact nature of the new social forms, and whether they connect with living Indigenous communal traditions or might be shaped by cultural holdovers from the past, will depend on specific circumstances, both national and regional. The question of regional differences in building the commune is addressed in the next chapter, which deals with an Andean commune in Venezuela near the Colombian border.

3

A Commune Called "Che": A Socialist Holdout in the Venezuelan Andes

A big fluffy dog. That is all Simón Bolívar got out of the Andean people when he went there looking for recruits and supplies at the time of the independence wars. The dog, named Nevado, entered the history books, but the coolness of Andean Venezuelans to Bolívar's project did not. A population of small farmers who owned their land, the region's campesinos were not willing to sign up for just any abstract proposal that involved much risk and unclear objectives. Moreover, these highland communities were not so leader-oriented: in one of the stories told about Bolívar's visit, the hero of Venezuelan independence got the dog because he asked to be shown their leader!

Just as the independence struggle had different resonances in the Andes, so too does Venezuela's project of communal socialism. The region is home to one of the most successful communes in the country, and, like other working communes, this one has a solid productive basis (a chocolate factory and coffee cooperative) and is run by experienced cadres. However, the Che Guevara Commune is markedly different from others that sprung up in response to Hugo Chávez's call to build communes as "the basic cells of socialism." More methodical, cautious, and pragmatic, the communards in these hillsides have built their project little by little, organizing their communities around the production and processing of two labor-intensive cash crops and the know-how they have acquired from cross-border migration.

The Che Guevara Commune is far removed from the bustle of Venezuela's huge coastal cities. You reach it by following a steep winding road from the shores of Lake Maracaibo into La Culata National Park. Lush vegetation and tall *bucare* trees provide good shade for coffee and cacao, which have only begun to be farmed in recent decades in this region, due to the migration triggered by the construction of the Pan-American Highway along the lake's perimeter in the 1950s. Many of the migrants in the area come from neighboring Colombia, bringing their traditions of hard work and, just as often, the political consciousness of veteran leftists fleeing persecution.

Such was the case of Neftalí Vanegaz, who came here in the early part of this century. A coffee grower who always maintained good relations with the leftist insurgency in his zone, Neftalí eventually fell under the suspicion of local paramilitary groups in Colombia. Those were the days of Álvaro Uribe's fascist offensive and the most aggressive phase of the U.S.-sponsored Plan Colombia. It was a time when suspicion was practically a death sentence. One day, facing down a pair of would-be assassins, Neftalí barely came away with his life. He wrested a pistol from one assailant, which jammed during the struggle, and then chased the other attacker away by brandishing the useless but menacing weapon. Having won this first battle in a stacked contest, the only thing to do now was flee. Neftalí made hasty tracks first to Medellín and later began an odyssey through El Salvador and Honduras that eventually took him to Venezuela's arid Guajira region.

Farmer Neftalí had fled with his young wife, Dioselina, and their infant son Felipe. It took them six days of walking through difficult terrain to get to the Guajira, where they had to live by fishing and hunting. In one difficult moment, they even ate a rare tapir. Life was hard in that sunbaked region, not the least because of mosquito-borne illnesses. After two years, they pressed on. Once they got to the highlands around Lake Maracaibo, it felt more like home. The region resembled Neftalí's mountainous birthplace in Colombia. The family set up a small farm, which later became the core of the Colimir cooperative in 2004, when Chávez first initiated the drive to make cooperatives. The farm would also become the keystone of the Che Guevara Commune.

From the torment of war, and having survived a dire crossing, the fugitive Vanegaz family ended up in the storm of Venezuela's socialist construction. A quick learner with revolutionary experience in his blood, the son, Felipe, would grow up in the fascinating context of the Bolivarian Process. Felipe and both his parents would ultimately become important communal leaders.

COFFEE AND INDEPENDENCE

Coffee and cacao production have a special relation to Venezuelan independence. It was cacao that lined the pockets of rich aristocratic planters in the country two centuries ago (called "grandes cacaos" for that reason). Emboldened by their wealth, with egos inflated by this export crop, the colony's cacao planters felt they were second to none in the metropolis and hence worthy of independence. Yet cacao was a crop that relied on enslaved people's labor, and the three waves of independence wars changed the demographics of the fledgling republic. With many enslaved people being freed or freeing themselves during this tumultuous epoch, growing cacao became less viable. This meant that, after independence, the new republic's main cash crop became coffee, which requires intense work but can be cultivated by families. Agricultural production in post-independence Venezuela often just shifted on the same plantation: from cacao in the lowlands to highland coffee cultivation.[1]

Today, in a similar way, the fallout from Chavismo's revolutionary advances, and especially the blockade imposed by the United States, has driven many Venezuelans back to coffee growing. This makes for a telling historical echo between what happened in the wake of the first independence struggle and the blowback from what could be called the second attempt at independence two hundred years later—this time from world capitalism. The key agricultural input for coffee growing is simply the elbow grease that family producers can provide. Yet the product is as good as gold, since it can be turned into hard currency locally, in neighboring Colombia, or in the international market. This is a clue as to why a small coffee-growing cooperative that lived through innumerable difficulties following its founding in 2004 would become the backbone of one of the country's flagship communes.

THE COLIMIR COOPERATIVE

A group of us from Caracas are visiting the Che Guevara Commune to investigate its responses to the U.S.-imposed sanctions, with a special interest in the innovative organization of labor and novel production techniques applied in its highland coffee cooperative and lower-lying cocoa factory. The trip is surprisingly rapid, consisting of a short flight to Mérida's El Vigía airport and a two-hour drive along the Pan-American Highway, then up steep hillsides to the village of Rio Bonito Alto, in the Mesa Julia township. It feels as if we have been beamed up into the commune, suddenly finding ourselves face to face with the coffee-processing plant of the Colimir Cooperative, which is buzzing with activity, its cyclopean drying tumbler and huge rotating dryer in constant motion, all amid a persistent odor of burnt coffee and diesel fuel.

We are met by Neftalí's son Felipe, who emerges from the plant in stained work clothes and accompanied by his own lively three-year-old. He begins by explaining the vicissitudes of the cooperative since its founding. Despite his youth (in the Global

North, he would be considered Generation Z), Felipe is a person who believes firmly in industrialization, maintaining a strictly scientific approach to socialist construction. It is an attitude that, in my mind, resonates with certain facets of V. I. Lenin's thought (remember the slogan "Soviet power plus electrification!"[2]). Felipe also has a pragmatic approach to the social and organizational side of socialist construction. A communal project's *raison d'être*, he tells us, is always the real needs of the community; when such needs are felt and understood, the projects thrive. Conversely, communes and cooperatives lose ground when collective needs are not understood, with people becoming more individualistic and ultimately turning away from the project.

The recent history of communal construction at Mesa Julia bears out Felipe's thesis, with its decade and a half of ups and downs being conditioned by the perceived needs of the local population. After Neftalí founded it in 2004, the Colimir coffee-processing cooperative virtually disappeared when the state corporation Café Venezuela set up shop in the zone and began buying coffee from local producers a few years later. People followed Chávez's lead in almost everything at that time, as it was laid out in the weekly television program *Aló Presidente*. This meant that by the end of 2006, when the official discourse began turning away from the cooperative model, many people around the country began to perceive the earlier drive as a mere error. Most cooperatives at the time had either failed or simply ceased to produce, continuing to exist in a kind of bureaucratic limbo, making the whole initiative seem like a dead end.

Still, pressing economic necessity was never too far away, and when the global economic crisis hit in 2008, things got going again at Colimir. In the first years of the cooperative, members had organized "collective work Mondays"—that is, voluntary work sessions involving all associates—which were reborn in 2009. Tough times made for more solidarity in the community and the cooperative's leaders were able to channel people's spontaneous barn-raising efforts into something resembling Lenin's

Red Saturdays. Then came renewed interest from helpful sectors of the government and a trickle of funding from the Ministry of Science and Technology, which supported the cooperative in a project of cultivating coffee seedlings and funded some terracing of the area's hillsides.

This was also the time when Chávez, after a few years of mixed success in forming state-owned enterprises, sent out the more radical call to make communes. He said that communes, as coordinated foci of political and economic democracy, were to be the place where socialism was born. A group of militants in the Mesa Julia zone responded to the call by incorporating at first ten and later as many as fourteen *consejos comunales* to form the Che Guevara Commune. However, the Colimir cooperative, which would later become its main economic motor, initially maintained its identity separate from the umbrella figure of the commune. The slight trickle of government support became more substantial when a new funding body, the Consejo Federal de Gobierno, helped finance the productive unit's infrastructure. Membership then boomed, reaching almost one hundred associates, only to fall away when the building project and the money associated with it ran out.

The hardest period for the coffee producers at Colimir came with the COVID pandemic and the country's severe economic crisis. Fuel shortages made drying the beans nearly impossible, and production came to a complete halt. When the Consejo Federal de Gobierno reached out and offered to help, the cooperativists researched solutions, discovering that coffee drying was being done elsewhere by burning the coffee husk itself, thereby drastically reducing dependence on diesel fuel. They also learned that the equipment to do so could be bought in Colombia. It was a triumphant day when these novel machines, financed by the Consejo Federal, arrived to Colimir's hillside coffee-processing plant, and were received by the communards. Thus, in the first months of 2021, a light shone at the end of the tunnel for a cooperative hard hit by U.S. sanctions, and yet held together by the social glue of pressing necessity and the firm mettle of its resilient communards.

COMMUNAL CURRENCY

As mentioned above, coffee in this zone is as good as money, and, at a certain point in the history of the Che Guevara Commune, it became so explicitly. This was during the two-year period when Colimir issued its own currency, called the *cafeto*, and made it equal in value to one kilo of coffee. We learn about this coffee-as-currency project when seated inside Colimir's small, comfortable business office, where Felipe has taken us to escape the persistent humming of the drying machines and diesel generator. This is where the cooperative manages its financial operations, which during those two years relied on an innovative local currency. The rise and fall of the cafeto at the Che Guevara Commune is a story worth telling for its insights into communal production, especially the importance of breaking the straitjacket of commodity exchange, while showing the real difficulties of such an attempt.

The economist Hyman Minsky used to say that anybody can *create* money; the problem lies in getting it *accepted.*[3] However, getting people to accept the cafeto was not especially difficult for the communards at Colimir, given the gravity of the economic crisis at the time. Runaway inflation, a product of economic attacks and an import-dependent economy, was systematically pulverizing the value of the Venezuelan bolívar, while the use of the U.S. dollar was illegal. This made people open to trying a new currency. Moreover, campesinos in the area were already measuring value with coffee. They would price a motorcycle or pair of boots in terms of kilos of coffee, using this as a shared base from which to speak about something's worth in a way that remained relatively stable over time.

By issuing the cafeto, the Colimir cooperative was thus in some basic sense just formalizing what people were already doing spontaneously. When producers came from around the region to the administrative offices of Colimir to sell their harvest, they were met with a "general equivalent" that was both familiar and new. The cooperative bought coffee from its associates and other producers most often with a digital version of the cafeto—they even developed their own Android app for it—but sometimes also with paper bills. Additionally, the cooperative made loans in cafetos, since small growers in the area always need financial support during times of planting and harvesting. At one point, there were some 17,000 cafetos in circulation, backed by an equal quantity of coffee stored at Colimir.

Felipe, pragmatic and always thinking about the future, looks back at that time with a critical perspective. Creating a local currency solved a problem, but it was not in itself a socialist measure. "The cafeto was more reliable than the Venezuelan bolívar, because it maintained its exchange value over time," he explains. "Since the dollar did not circulate freely at the time—it was illegal—the cafeto was perfect." However, he indicates that people also found the new currency confusing, since rising coffee prices meant that debts contracted in cafetos had to be paid back with nominally greater sums. Hence, the cooperative found it difficult to collect loans it had advanced to local producers. "Unlike many other enterprises, we were not victims of the devaluation," Felipe says. "Yet we lost money because we lent to people who did not pay us back."

Working in the office today is the cooperative's financial coordinator, Yeini Urdaneta. It is her responsibility to juggle the community's numerous requests for economic support (to help cover the costs of births, medical visits, funerals, and so on), but she also had to manage the loans to producers and the problem of unpaid cafeto debt. Despite the difficulties, she agrees with Felipe that "the overall experience of the cafeto was good, because it allowed us to circumvent hyperinflation." Urdaneta proudly shows us one of the cafeto bills—printed with color xerox—that she keeps folded in her wallet as a memento, along with a still crisp mimeographed sheet of paper explaining how the cafeto was to be used. Tellingly, if somewhat quixotically, the norms begin by saying that the cafeto project is meant to "satisfy collective needs."

It is not surprising that the cafeto experience was a mixed one and a source of ongoing reflection at the Che Guevara Commune. In capitalist society, money expresses socially validated labor time. The value it represents is universal—you can obtain any commodity with money—but it results from private labor activities. Money fetishism derives from this contradictory situation: a currency has real buying power, but this power comes from dispersed private labor activities that leave no trace on the bills. Insofar as communes attempt to make labor something valued in itself—especially for the use-values it generates—instead of simply geared toward anonymous exchange-value, it is understandable that they will turn to halfway measures such as barter or, in this case, the use of local currencies more closely connected to concrete labor activities and their products. The final evaluation of these transitory measures will itself depend on the course of the overall transition toward a post-capitalist society, of which these vanguard communes hope to be the initial cells.

The Chocolate Factory

Apart from the Colimir coffee cooperative, the Che Guevara Commune is home to a sizable cacao-processing plant. On our second day at Mesa Julia, we drop down some five hundred meters along a steep concrete path to visit its offices, factory spaces, and greenhouses, all dedicated to the different stages of chocolate making. This second productive project of the commune got started some five years after the Colimir coffee cooperative. Yet, the comrades working here represent the vanguard of the commune, if not in a productive sense, at least in an organizational one. The main impulse for organizing the *consejos comunales* in the zone, and later the Che Guevara Commune, came from the circle of this cacao plant—the Che Guevara Socialist Production Enterprise (or Che Guevara EPS, for its Spanish-language acronym). It was also that group that gave the commune its distinguished name.

The Che Guevara EPS's main spokesperson is Ernesto Cruz, who migrated from Colombia decades ago for economic reasons. Soft-spoken, studious, and hardworking, the now forty-something community organizer is seated at a desk in the plant's small office, explaining how the commune got its revolutionary name. "My aunt Olga Veracruz, who was politically formed in the midst of the war in Colombia, was the one who proposed calling the commune 'Che Guevara.'" Ernesto tells us how Olga encouraged people to organize first in communal councils and later in the commune, proposing that Che Guevara's conception of solidarity should be the guiding principle for the region's communards. "That is why we call ourselves the 'Che Guevara Commune.'"

Ernesto's revolutionary aunt belonged to the old leftist tradition. Having followed her nephew's footsteps by settling in the zone, she organized reading groups with local women and was the moral force behind a local newspaper with a leftist vision. However, naming the commune Che Guevara was met with some resistance in this conservative region, where religion is a cultural mainstay. Evidence of dissent from the community can still be seen in the cocoa plant's lunchroom. The space is dominated by a large Che Guevara painting based on Alberto Korda's famous photo showing the young revolutionary with a leonine mane and uplifted eyes (Korda airbrushed them that way). Next to it, someone has discreetly pasted a Psalm of David! Juxtaposing psalm and painting might indeed represent a struggle in the region, but because the Bible verses speak of "the beauty of people living harmoniously together," they resonate well with both the commune's overall project and Che's commitment to solidarity and self-sacrifice.

Fiction tells us that visiting a chocolate factory should be an adventure full of mystery and surprises. In Roald Dahl's classic story, the most telling surprise is how labor is carried out.

Chocolate-making depends on the "enlightened slavery" of Oompa Loompas, who lived on a sad diet of caterpillars until factory owner Wonka "rescued" them from the bad food and dangerous predators of Loompaland. In this way, *Charlie and the Chocolate Factory* offers readers a *deus ex machina* solution to the problem of wage labor and tries to cover up capitalist exploitation. In the Che Guevara EPS, there is a different, less mystified solution to the problem of exploitation, though from a capitalist perspective it is just as surprising. Here, exploitative and alienated labor is overcome through the ample application of democracy to all stages and steps of the production process. The surprise comes because in capitalism we are led to believe that this is all impossible, since supposedly workers need bosses and do not understand producing.

Workplace democracy and self-organized labor is what is most valued by Zulay Montilla, who works alongside Ernesto in the plant's administrative area. "This is direct social property," she tells us in reference to Chávez's distinction between *direct* social property, which is self-managed by communities, and the *indirect* form that is state-run. "There are fifteen workers at the plant, and we are organized according to four areas: administration, accounting, production, and training. However, more important than the structure of the organization here is that there is no president, no manager, no boss. Decisions are made collectively in assembly with equal participation from all workers." Anticipating a question that goes back centuries in this region, Zulay explains: "When people ask, 'Who is the boss?' we tell them that there is no chief here, that everyone's voice counts equally. . . . But it can be hard for them to understand this new form of organization." A few centuries ago, perhaps, she would have sent those same inquirers packing with a big fluffy dog.

COMMUNE VS. CRISIS

Ernesto's family has something like revolutionary discipline in its bones. Organization, planning, and a seriousness that verges on somberness are the most noticeable characteristics of their modus operandi in both work and in life. Asked how they are, even casually, family members generally respond: "We are ready for war!" War is meant figuratively, of course. Nevertheless, they brought this determined attitude with them from Colombia. It is the ethic of revolutionaries in that war-ridden country, and it is all about hitting the ground running. On arriving to a new territory, one begins by recruiting militants, building a cell, and, of course, producing food for one's people.

All of this was foreign to the Venezuelan locals when the Cruz family arrived at Mesa Julia some twenty years ago. Then food was abundant, and Chávez's revolutionary government seemed capable of doing all the necessary organizing and mobilization. But then came a war-like situation: the country was nearly brought to its knees economically, first by the "economic war" (2014–16) and later by the sanctions (2016–present). In this new context, the Cruz family's attitude began to get more traction. This is in part because the commune they built has won credibility by providing the community with schooling, cooking gas distribution, and transportation, at a time when the state is no longer willing or able to do so. For example, the commune constructed a small school, painted with bright colors and stenciled numbers inside, in the upper region of Mesa Julia in what was formerly a state-run Mercal grocery store. They also repaired an old city bus to take people up and down the steep hillsides. For all these reasons, neighbors in the area are beginning to see the value of communal work and look to self-organization rather than top-down solutions to address their problems.

Ernesto is an atheist and, even in informal conversation, he frequently invokes Baruch Spinoza's philosophy to underpin his monistic-materialist approach to life and work. Yet, he says that there is one thing Christianity teaches that is a necessary supplement to revolutionary socialist ideology: *desprendimiento*, meaning both detachment and generosity. (Che Guevara's life embodied it too—for example, when he left the safe, stable existence he had in Cuba to fight in Congo and later Bolivia.) Just ten years ago, *desprendimiento* seemed to have nothing to do with Chavismo. They were like Lewis Carroll's proverbial raven and writing desk. In that golden era, the Bolivarian Revolution was literally the gift that kept on giving. It spewed out food, cars, and houses by the millions, to say nothing of the educational and health services it offered freely to the country's residents. What need, then, was there for sacrifice or self-denial? Fast forward to the present and the downfall of Chavismo's original social contract has started to cause massive shifts in allegiances. Those who believed that a revolution was just about receiving material goods have begun either falling by the wayside or eagerly seeking to join the privileged elites. Only those who had a grasp on the then esoteric concept of *desprendimiento*—often from some previous experience in revolutionary practice and ethics—could see the way forward without their vision being clouded by resentment or pain.

When Ernesto evaluates the current situation, in which the Che Guevara Commune has only the barest thread of state support and has had to pick up much of the slack in assisting the community, he is far less visceral than urban Chavistas who frequently speak as if they had had their favorite bone stolen by the crisis: "Chávez told us that the way to overcome capitalism is with the commune. Now, however, it often seems as if the state has lost sight of the communal project. It's a real problem, but we should be self-critical: many within the Bolivarian Process imagined that this revolution would have access to the oil resources forever. That was a bad calculation, and we are now trying to find our feet."

Ernesto looks to the future with measured optimism: "All this doesn't mean that Chávez's communal proposal was mistaken. Quite the contrary: we have to generate conditions to develop production and diversify, and experience shows that the commune is actually the way to do it. . . . In our effort to construct a new hegemony, it is important that we have been able to be self-sufficient in great measure. The EPS is producing chocolate and Colimir is producing coffee—those concrete achievements help people to not become demoralized." Before leaving, we visit the outdoor drying patio, where the cacao beans are spread out and raked under the sun, the greenhouse for seedlings (to improve the quality of local cacao trees), the fermentation sheds, and finally the clean, cool rooms where chocolate is poured into molds to make a marvelous array of bars and bonbons. The inebriating smell of chocolate permeates every space of the building, in a kind of olfactory counterpoint to Ernesto's sober reflections.

Grassroots Internationalism

Being ready for war takes on a direct, more literal meaning in the last days of our trip. Word has gotten out that a group of foreigners is visiting, and certain unspecified actors in Tucaní, where our hotel is located, are said to be shadowing us with a view to a holdup or kidnapping. This is hardly surprising, since the whole frontier area is rife with criminal groups and some branches of the police have fallen into crime. Felipe, who meets us with a worried look on his face, has brought this alarming news. He tells us that we need to abandon the hotel and spend our last night in the commune's bunkroom. There is a small militia here that guards the buildings and grounds (this protection is needed because stealing crops has become common during the crisis). They were initially formed as part of the Bolivarian Reserve, but later, as that project began to lose direction, the armed organization Tupamaros offered them additional training. It is almost certain that the militia also receives some help and training from across the border.

I know the context of the Bolivarian militias well, having spent a year in the university's reserve when I first arrived in the country fifteen years ago. The ranks of our volunteer battalion were mostly filled by cleaners, janitors, and drivers at the university.

They were all authentic Chavistas, totally committed to the country and to the revolution. Few professors or administrators were willing to take part, since they thought volunteering in a popular militia was beneath them and threatened their status as professionals. Old habits die hard in the middle classes. As one of the few who broke with the professorial ranks, I was welcomed wholeheartedly by these *milicianos*, who showed themselves to be true internationalists and, between our long hours spent in drills, asked questions about left movements in the world to the bookish foreigner who had appeared in their midst.

This was light-years away in the heyday of Chavismo, when all of us were focused on defending the project, since its anti-imperialism and recently declared socialist objectives would almost surely bring about, we thought, a U.S. invasion. Up in the commune's bunkroom, I encounter that same kind of revolutionary spirit and grassroots internationalism again. The *miliciana* charged with taking care of us is a woman named Herrera, who sleeps there with her three beautiful children. She offers us warm pieces of pork and frisbee-sized *arepas* that we wash down with generous cups of sugary coffee. After the lights go out in the commune's bunkroom, with my belly full and sleep beginning to waft over me, I notice a wooden rifle is laid out on the bunk above Herrera. The guerrilla across the border uses these for training. I fall into slumber thinking that the authentic article is surely stashed elsewhere.

The next day, we set off early for the El Vigia airport accompanied by Felipe and his partner. Our backpacks are full of chocolate and coffee, while our minds are fairly spinning from the generosity, solidarity, and commitment of a group of communards who more than live up to their project's revolutionary name. The memories and mementos make me think we came away from this Andean redoubt with better luck than Bolívar. Yet the best gift we received from these communards is surely what they have taught us by example. There is clearly much to be learned from the internationalist attitude that exists in this commune, which was founded largely by Colombian migrants, under the auspices of the ideas of Marx, Chávez, and Che. It points to the importance of having a rich exchange of ideas and practices across borders in the name of the common goal of emancipation. This interchange of ideas also mirrors the process by which the communal idea was born in Venezuela, as we will see in the next chapter.

4

Mészáros and Chávez: The Philosopher and the Llanero

It is a strange and interesting story how the longstanding and ultimately two-way relationship between revolutionary Venezuelan politician Hugo Chávez and Hungarian philosopher István Mészáros came to exist. It is a tale of elective affinities. On one side, we have a kid who grew up in the Venezuelan *llanos* region in a household too poor to buy tableware. As a boy living with his grandmother, the young Hugo sold candy in the streets but wanted to play baseball, inspired by a namesake pitcher (El Látigo Chávez) on the team Magallanes. He entered the armed forces hoping to become a *pelotero*, but soon discovered that the army offered him a school for studying politics and history, along with a privileged vantage point from which to observe the injustices and contradictions of Venezuelan society. On the other side of the story, we have Mészáros, a full generation older than the former Venezuelan president. Mészáros grew up poor in Budapest, worked with Georg Lukács, emigrated to Italy following the 1956 uprising, then moved to England, where he spent most of the rest of his life.

What made Mészáros's life so fascinating, and relevant to issues of socialist construction, was that, having seen both sides of the Cold War, he came to perceive both "real socialism" and twentieth-century capitalism as two variants of the same system. He called this the *capital system*. The basic commonality among most countries of both the East and West in the twentieth century was the extraction of surplus labor from workers who did not control their own work processes. Living in England in the late 1960s and early '70s, Mészáros witnessed how the shared capital system entered a profound crisis.[1] On the one hand, the countries of the West implemented neoliberal reforms inspired by the theories of Friedrich Hayek and Milton Friedman. These newly coined neoliberal policies allowed the West to kick the can down the street, riding out a crisis it could not definitively resolve. On the other hand, in the Eastern Bloc countries, the same structural crisis would be the preamble to the implosion of post-revolutionary systems that because of their hybrid nature— they continued to extract surplus labor from workers but could not apply the same economic pressures as the strictly speaking capitalist system—were unable to ride out the crisis with even the limited success of Ronald Reagan and Margaret Thatcher's governments.

This was still the age of "three worlds," and from the privileged position of living and working in two of them, Mészáros developed his key ideas. The most important of these was that capital was essentially a metabolic system, dependent on a vertical division of labor over which it has command. Capital's metabolic system could manifest itself as capitalism *per se*, as it did in the countries of the West, but it could also take on variant forms in post-revolutionary societies. To refer to the latter, Mészáros used the terms *Soviet capital system*, *post-revolutionary capital system*, and sometimes *post-capitalist capital system*. His claim was that the capital system's hierarchical, anti-democratic metabolism and its extraction of surplus labor—all in a social context where things dominate people—went on existing in what was falsely known as "real" or "actually existing" socialism. A corollary to this thesis was that the only way to overcome the whole capital system, not just the outright *capitalist form* of the capital system, was through a radical reorganization of society in which workers themselves consciously control production in a profoundly democratic way. Faced with the system's crisis, what was needed was not less socialism but more! Self-managed production and the existence of substantive democracy at all levels of this alternative society were the key features of what Mészáros called the *communal system*. He saw it as the only viable, sustainable alternative to the capital system.

The affinities with Chávez's ideas and policies should be clear enough from this brief introduction alone. As is well known, Chávez had a firm belief in substantive democracy as the centerpiece and mainspring of socialism; he wagered on community councils and other forms of self-organization to emancipate the Venezuelan people ("Only the people will liberate the people," Chávez said on numerous occasions); and he opted in the end for a communal system to build socialism (echoing Mészáros's claim that not a "less socialist" but "more socialist" socialism was needed in the twenty-first century). All these features make for a striking isomorphism between the two figures, despite their widely divergent backgrounds and upbringings. As it turned out, Chávez would mobilize his followers and significant resources with a hypothesis that was in great measure based on the Hungarian philosopher's approach to the socialist transition.

How Chávez Got to the Commune

To understand how Chávez could be so open to Mészáros's influence as to turn to the commune as the main strategic element in socialist construction, it is useful to look at the previous trajectory of experimentation during the Bolivarian Process in the area of production, including the vicissitudes of such experiments owing to their mixed results. One of the first attempts to change the overall nature of Venezuela's economy after the revolution was the nationwide drive to form cooperatives. This initiative, which started around 2003, involved a special legal framework and huge mobilization of resources, mostly drawn from oil profits during this boom decade. With enthusiastic mass participation that was typical of the Bolivarian Process in its heyday, cooperatives began popping up all around Venezuela, proudly displaying a logo consisting of two pine trees standing side by side inside a yellow circle. There were a range of service cooperative projects, including taxi, hotdog, and haircutting cooperatives, as well as productive cooperatives, such as those devoted to agriculture and different forms of manufacturing and light industry.

The gamut of cooperatives organized in those years exhibited varied levels of concreteness. Human beings are products of their contexts, and, given the desperate situation of longstanding exclusion that most Venezuelans had experienced, it is not surprising that many people formed cooperatives that existed only on paper, since by registering a cooperative, you could get access to state contracts and grants. But there were also registered cooperatives that really existed, operated by flesh and blood workers using tangible means of production, which still fell short of being true cooperatives. For all intents and purposes, many were just ordinary capitalist businesses, with a whole structure of bosses and hierarchy hiding behind cooperative laws. Very quickly—most likely relying on advisors and on his reading—Chávez came to understand that cooperatives could be problematic; despite collective ownership, they are still private property. Cooperatives are essentially a kind of *collective* private property, with their own adversarial relationships with other enterprises, including other cooperatives, with which they compete, and with society at large.

Around 2006, in the very years that Chávez proposed that the country pursue socialism as a goal, he started to experiment with various forms of state property, usually in some mixed format. This was the epoch when *co-management* and the so-called *social production enterprises* were buzzwords of the day. People with a

Marxist background will note that the concept of a *social produc-tion enterprise* is flawed in that all capitalist businesses rely on social production. In capitalism, there is a basic contradiction in that capitalist *production* is always *social*, meaning that a capital-ist business employs a plurality of people and might have a web of suppliers reaching around the globe. Yet capitalist *property* is private and "antisocial"—it tends toward ever greater concentra-tion in fewer hands. After becoming aware of this problematic nomenclature, Chávez changed his discourse and began referring instead to *social property enterprises* (EPSs, for their Spanish-language acronym).

This epoch had its fascinating moments, but it was also quite bumpy. There were some notable successes. For a few years, the cooking oil business Industrias Diana was a flagship state-owned enterprise that operated under the "co-management" modality. Its moment of glory was when the workers themselves ran the business, but then some army officers were brought in to direct the production and things took a turn for the worse. The aluminum factory in Venezuela's Guayana region, Alcasa, run by the now disappeared Carlos Lanz, was another interesting experiment. The 2006 film *5 Factories*, made by Oliver Ressler and Dario Azzellini, offers a window into some of these experi-ments, focusing exclusively on success stories.[2] Nevertheless, if one looks at the period as a whole, the failures and shortcomings of Venezuela's state-run enterprises (often due to problems of bureaucratization, as with the Diana oil factory) are also obvious.

After this trajectory of economic experiments—which in a way represents an accelerated replay of twentieth-century socialist experimentation in microeconomics—Chávez became interested in an alternative model for socialist production. In just five years, the Bolivarian Process had first tried cooperatives and then state property, experiencing the limits of both formats. Now the Process attempted to move forward with a new model, something that transcended these constraints: the commune. When Chávez finally turned to the commune around 2009 and 2010, he was partly inspired by Chinese communes—and said so, brandishing a small book about the commune of Chiliying. He took his lead, however, from the philosopher Mészáros. Indeed, Chávez was so inspired by Mészáros that he made his communal system the center of Venezuela's efforts in socialist construction and mobilized huge resources for a project that was profoundly influenced by the Hungarian thinker's ideas.

The Missing Link

We have mentioned the principal affinities between Chávez's and Mészáros's thought and pointed to some reasons for their intellectual synchronicity. Yet, how did the actual, concrete connection between two people of such disparate backgrounds come about? The link had a name: Jorge Giordani, a Venezuelan university professor who was a friend of both Chávez and Mészáros. As is often the case with historically important friendships, Giordani came to know first Mészáros and later Chávez through a series of fortuitous accidents. A longstanding leftist, Giordani began his university career studying engineering and planning in Caracas but later continued his education in Italy and England, where he got to know Mészáros and his family when they lived in an apartment that overlooked the Wimbledon tennis courts.[3]

On returning to Venezuela, Giordani continued his academic work in the Center for Development Studies, forming there an informal team that called itself the Dead Planners Society, inspired by the Robin Williams film. This left-leaning group dealt with issues related to planning and development. Giordani had come back to a country in tumoil. The 1989 Caracazo massacre and the neoliberal adjustments that provoked it had made for a crisis that shook even the ivory tower, drawing sympathy from the country's progressive academics. On March 26, 1993, the professors Francisco Mieres and Adina Bastides, who were part of the Dead Planners group, decided to visit Chávez in Yare, where he was imprisoned following the failed 1992 insurrection.

There was space for only a few visitors, and the first chance to accompany the pair was given to Héctor Navarro, who demurred, joking that he did not like going to prison "even as a visitor." This gave Giordani an opening, though he was initially denied entry by the guards. Finally, the prison authorities let him in, and he found himself among such a large, noisy gathering, that it seemed more like a chaotic party than a prison cell.

When the time came to leave, at around 5 p.m.—just a few minutes before closing—Giordani got up to go. Just then he heard Chávez call out "Professor!" He thought that Chávez was hailing Mieres, but the imprisoned soldier was clear: "No, it's about you." It was then that Chávez told Giordani that he wanted him to be his thesis advisor for a degree in political science he was pursuing while in prison. When Chávez said he had tried to contact the economic planning specialist before the 1992 military uprising, Giordani's first reaction was relief: "Thank God you didn't get in touch with me earlier or I would be in prison here with you." Yet he agreed to be Chávez's thesis tutor. This is how this important friendship began, with Giordani visiting Chávez weekly in prison (until the authorities stopped them), where they talked about Antonio Gramsci, Karl Marx, and, of course, Mészáros.

Giordani had been interested in Mészáros's ideas since meeting him in England. Now, back in Venezuela, he became, in his words, a kind of "conveyor belt," transmitting information about what was happening there to the Hungarian philosopher and, more generally, serving as a link between Mészáros and Chávez during the 1990s. One important task that Giordani took on was getting Mészáros's huge work from 1995, *Beyond Capital*, translated into Spanish. Initially, the Dead Planners Society attempted a collective translation, with each member taking responsibility for a different section of the thousand-page volume. It did not go well. Yet, Giordani had a chance encounter with a high school friend called Eduardo Gasca, who agreed to translate the whole text. This is how Venezuela came to have the first translation into

Spanish of this major work, published by Vadell Hermanos Press. (As it turned out, Mészáros was very pleased with the translation, finding Gasca's version of Attila József's poems better than the existing translations that had been done some years earlier, directly from the Hungarian!)

MÉSZÁROS AND THE COMMUNAL SYSTEM

Chávez frequently brandished the hefty tome of *Beyond Capital* in official meetings and in television appearances, telling his ministers to read and study it. He also sometimes gave copies to foreign dignitaries (including Mahmoud Ahmadinejad, who was clearly disconcerted to receive a copy translated by Iranian communists). On the website *Todo Chávez*, which has all of Chávez's speeches, one can chart how references to Mészáros first appear in Chávez's reflections in 2003 and later enter the discourse with greater and greater frequency, up until the president's untimely death ten years later.[4] Chávez typically mentions book titles and a few catchphrases, such as *social metabolism*, *the challenges of our time*, *irreversibility*, *humanly rewarding transition*, and constantly encourages study of Mészáros's work. But the references are, in fact, sparse. So, what exactly were Mészáros's key ideas and how did they influence Chávez?

Mészáros's main discovery was that the "capital system" is not equivalent to capitalism. To underpin his focus on *capital* as the decisive Marxist category rather than *capitalism*, the philosopher could point to the very title of Marx's most important work (it is called *Capital*, not *Capitalism*) and the first volume's often mistranslated subtitle (*The Process of Production of Capital*, not, as Frederick Engels rendered it, *A Critical Analysis of Capitalist Production*). Mészáros's claim was that Marx's main object of study, *capital*, embodies a diffuse, all-pervasive metabolism. This cannot be reduced to a scenario in which greedy capitalists exploit workers through the extraction of surplus value, but rather consists of a whole range of more fundamental ("second order") mediations that are imposed by capital's logic on human beings' ("first order") relations to nature and other humans. By way of these mediations, capital generates and constantly reproduces an integral system involving, on the one hand, alienated means of production, producers divorced from control over the production process, and a command of labor that works through externally imposed production goals; on the other hand, the capital system also shapes family relations, imposes money and its mystifying forms on an expanding range of social interactions, and generates alienated state-forms of administration and control.[5]

Mészáros's discovery about the all-embracing, organic capital system was not purely theoretical. His thesis had practical consequences that are observable in history, namely, that you can overcome the capitalist system and still reproduce what he called the "logic" or "metabolism" of capital. Mészáros made this clear when he wrote "Without capital, the capitalist is nothing [but the] relation obviously does not hold the other way around."[6] This is exactly what happened in the Soviet Union and other Eastern Bloc countries. These were indeed post-capitalist societies—not "state capitalist societies" as some critics have argued—but they continued to reproduce the key elements of the capital system, including laborers with no control over the production process (a hierarchical command over labor), production goals that were undemocratically imposed from above, alienated means of production, extraction of surplus labor, and state forms that corresponded to the alien objectification of labor.[7] The Soviet system was a *capital* system, even if not a *capitalist* one, because it shared these essential features. The narrowly capitalist features it lacked, most especially the economic pressure that capitalism puts on workers (who must work or starve), would at some point constitute a hindrance that impeded its ability to compete with the West's productivity. Thus, having maintained a top-down control of enterprises, Soviet leaders soon wanted to have its "twin brothers" in the form of free markets and full capitalist restoration.

Yet, Mészáros did not simply use his discovery to criticize the really existing socialism of the Eastern Bloc, under which he had lived. He also employed it as the basis for an alternative strategic proposal. In contrast to the failed attempts to overcome capital that were, on the one hand, real socialism and, on the other, evolutionist social democracy—Mészáros believed that they had a great deal in common—the Hungarian philosopher took it upon himself to write about the transition to what could represent a true, socialist alternative to the entire *capital* system. Building this viable alternative would be a huge challenge, and he never disguised its difficulties. (It was more difficult than going to Mars, Chávez said, summarizing Mészáros's claim.[8]) This task would require generating an integral, organic system that, just like the capital system, could reproduce itself and whose different elements mutually supported each other. It made no sense to overcome just one part of the capital system—say, the alienated means of production—without aiming at the whole, because the various components of the capital system all interpenetrated each other and could successfully resist any partial attempt to overcome them. What was needed was a holistic, comprehensive strategy, aimed at implementing a new organic system, the components of which were themselves mutually reinforcing.

¡COMUNA O NADA!

Mészáros saw this alternative system—the authentic socialist system—as essentially a communal one. He called it the *self-constituting communal system*. The Hungarian philosopher scoured the archives of both Marx's published work and his manuscripts to show that communal production had been what Marx had more or less consistently seen as the alternative to the capital system and its *post-festum* social production (an idea that was concealed by the usual statist reading of Marx but is evident to any careful reader).[9] This amounted to an interpretive, textual claim. Beyond this hermeneutic register, Mészáros worked to show that

the only way to restore control of production to direct producers, to overcome the market, to sideline the fetishistic forms of
commodities and money, and allow for sustainable production
with rationally established goals, in a way that is organic in the
sense that each part reinforces the rest, was through a communal
system. The obvious conclusion was that the commune constituted an "Archimedean point" for revolutionary social change
and the only viable historical alternative to capital's increasingly
destructive organic system. The communal system alone offers
"a framework of social metabolic exchange . . . usable by the individuals for securing their own ends."[10]

Mészáros reiterated this claim on various occasions. For
example, in an essay published in 2008 in *Monthly Review* that
elaborated on some key themes from *Beyond Capital*, we find
him claiming that the necessary alternative to capital's "ubiqui-
tously destructive system" was the communal mode of societal
reproduction, because "only the *communally organized system* is
capable of providing the overall framework for the continuing
development of the multifaceted and substantively equitable
constitutive parts of the socialist mode of integration of all
creative individual and collective forces into a *coherent whole* as
a historically viable *organic system of metabolic reproduction*."[11]
This passage is indeed labyrinthine, and it is, unfortunately, typical of Mészáros's theoretical exposition. However, its basic idea is
that, if the aim is to develop "rich social individuals," this kind of
self-realization could only be obtained through the "freely associated" producers that Marx talked about in *Capital* consciously
determining the nature, aims, and methods of their own work.

Communes provide a sustainable alternative precisely because
they are based on cooperation. The role of cooperation in promoting sustainability can be explained by considering the opposite
scenario. The capital system has conflict built into it, not only
the antagonism between different capitals competing with each
other, but also the structural conflict between capital and labor.
In the socialist alternative system, direct producers would take

on decision-making themselves, assuming responsibility for their self-determined objectives. But they cannot do this if they always find themselves with other social actors constantly pulling in the opposite direction, with opposing aims. Hence, the socialist alternative requires a *comprehensively cohesive social consciousness* that is amenable to workers' personal involvement in the control process and in decision-making about objectives.[12] Otherwise, adversarial relations and conflict between individuals and the collective will generate uncontrollable centrifugal forces that wreak havoc on society's coherence. This is the basis of Mészáros's claim that adversarial relations—built into the logic of the capital system (antagonism both among capitals and between capital and labor)—can only be overcome through a communal system, based on cooperation.

The essence of this new kind of society, in the words of Ricardo Antunes, is that "its vital functions—those that control its system of social metabolism—are effectively exercised autonomously by the freely-associated producers and not by an external, extraneous body in control of those functions."[13] What else but a commune, an organ of both production and internal democracy, can exercise this self-governed control of production? In fact, the ideas of Mészáros, whose point of departure is a thorough command of both Marxism and philosophy and whose presentation is often quite complex, not to say convoluted, could be summed up with Chávez's slogan, *Commune or Nothing!* The main claim of Mészáros's huge thousand-page codex is that only a *communal system* can replace the destructive, alienating, and dangerous *capital system*. In *Beyond Capital*, this claim pervades the whole work, but it is laid out most explicitly in chapter 19, "The Communal System and the Law of Value."

THE STATE MUST ALSO GO

In the recent Marvel film *Black Widow* (2021), there appears the curious figure of the Red Guardian—a Soviet "super-soldier" turned pariah by the name of Alexei Shostakov. Interestingly, he represents a kind of Soviet dissident without being an anti-communist defector or right-wing dissenter. The Red Guardian's sin, by his own admission, is that he still believes in the "withering away of the state." Leaving aside Marvel's bizarre post-Cold War politics (which seem equally unable to leave behind the Cold War as to revive it), the presence of a leftist Soviet dissenter in a mainstream movie is curious. How should we understand it? One reading would be that today communism is so weak that any reference to it seems simply quaint or nostalgic—mere entertainment! However, more optimistically, the space given to the Red Guardian's "ultra-leftism" on the big screen could be taken as a symptom of the growing awareness among both screenwriters and the public that some alternative is needed both to the capitalist system and the failed Soviet one.

In a world where social democrats and old Stalinists alike cling to the state form for dear life, Mészáros could be seen as the Red Guardian's kindred spirit, keenly interested in the problem of the state and postulating its overcoming as the non-negotiable core of Marxist political theory. Though opposed to the state and committed to its ultimate abolition, Mészáros was always careful to avoid any voluntarism in this respect. The state could not be abolished by decree but only transcended through the long-term activity of the proletariat in a "permanent" social revolution. Doing so, he wrote, required the proletariat's "active involvement in the revolutionary process itself on a painfully long time-scale."[14] Only the proletariat's activity in generating a new metabolism and normalizing "the spontaneous action of the laws of [a socialist] social economy" could lead to the state's final withering away.

Though taking state power is an important step in any revolution, especially at first, there remains the task of restructuring the social metabolism: the totality of social practice. In the effort to generate this new social metabolism, there could be some help in the form of guarantees from a new political form (a workers' state or popular government), which should provide a framework that promotes new, non-adversarial modes of control. However, the real focus of transformative work must operate at a grassroots level and be carried out by labor itself, on a material terrain that is quite different from normal politics, all of it aiming to turn labor's new mode of activity into a kind of spontaneous "second nature." This is where the commune comes in. Since the rule of capital is essentially "economic not political in character," it "cannot be broken at the political level."[15] This means that after the first step of intervening in or overthrowing the actual, immediate state formation, there lies the strategic project of suppressing the rule of capital itself and eventually all possible state forms.[16] Only implementing this new logic on the grassroots level—in communes and other self-governed spaces—in a way that extends throughout all of society could, in turn, render all state forms unnecessary.

The whole process is extremely complex. For this reason, Mészáros likens the transition to socialism to a complicated project of house remodeling. He tells the story of how Johann Wolfgang von Goethe's father rebuilt the family house from the inside, since building codes in eighteenth-century Frankfurt prevented new houses from overhanging the street. To maintain the breadth of the spaces where his family had resided, Goethe's father worked floor by floor, "rebuilding the inherited edifice in its entirety."[17] For Mészáros, this tricky process serves as a kind of model for the socialist transition. Many Marxists have fallen into the trap of presenting the transition as a brief and relatively simple process of kicking out the capitalists and destroying "their" state. Having witnessed the dilemmas and challenges of various post-revolutionary projects, Mészáros felt that even Marx himself, caught up in polemics with his contemporaries and focusing on the broadest outlines of the socialist project, had failed to address the complexity of the transition.[18] In reality, capital, wage labor, and the state were integral parts of the complex capital system, which would have to be dismantled from within, without any one element capable of completely disappearing through fiat decisions, however well intentioned.

V. I. Lenin, who is famous for saying that in any revolution the key question is state power, was in fact right to point to the state's centrality in maintaining the organic capital system in which labor and capital are the other main pillars.[19] Mészáros expressed this idea by saying that the state was the system's "mediation par excellence . . . combining around a political focus the totality of internal relations."[20] However, since all three components—state, wage labor, and capital—are profoundly intertwined, you cannot simply "smash the bourgeois state" leaving labor's dependence on capital fundamentally unaltered. Labor's dependence on capital is the material basis of the state and is in a profound sense what calls it into being. Such dependence can only be changed through a "radical restructuring of the totality of social reproductive processes," like the progressive rebuilding of an inherited house from the inside.[21] Given this interdependence, the withering away of the state after taking power depends on the challenging, drawn-out process of making both capital and dependent labor wither away: "The vicious circle of labour being locked into its structural dependency [on] capital, on the one hand, and into a subordinate position at the level of political decision-making by an alien state power on the other, can only be broken if the producers progressively cease to reproduce the material supremacy of capital. This they can only do by radically challenging the hierarchical structural division of labor."[22]

In this restructuring project, Mészáros envisioned a long-term social process in which labor would have the protagonist role. The imposed *division* of labor would be replaced by a consciously self-determined *organization* of labor by the workers themselves.[23] The process required was "possible only if all controlling functions of the social metabolism . . . are progressively appropriated and positively exercised by the associated producers."[24] Consider, now, these features: the appropriation of production by workers, all controlling functions exercised by associated producers, and the reintegration of administrative functions into the community. What is the basic social form indicated here? These features point to a particular social form: the commune, or at least this is how Chávez understood it, who was fond of Mészáros's description of the Goethe family house and referenced it in his *Aló Presidente* programs. Admirably, Mészáros had laid out the way forward for socialist construction, never denying its complexity. No wonder, then, that Chávez praised Mészáros as the "Pathfinder of Socialism," highlighting his work in developing a theory of the socialist transition, for which Marx had not left a detailed theoretical account!

VENEZUELAN COMMUNES AS CELLS OF A NEW SOCIALIST SYSTEM

Venezuelan communes embody a new social metabolism of a qualitatively different type, with their self-determined control of production, achieved through assemblies and other grassroots organizational forms. At the same time, these communes prefigure in a concrete way the democratic decision-making processes that can substitute for the state, ultimately abolishing its separate legality and administration.

Some of the characteristics of the emergent social system can be seen—and one can look at their different degrees of expression in the communes spread across Venezuela's extended territory—by simply putting a negation sign in front of what Mészáros identified as the key features of the capital system. If the capital system alienates the means of production from workers, the commune makes those means belong to the community. If capital's hierarchical division of labor requires that workers are controlled by command structures from above, the commune makes all production methods and goals the result of democratic decision-making, with capital's externally imposed production goals replaced by internally self-determined ones. (In what was essentially his last testament, the famous "Golpe de Timón" speech, Chávez quoted Mészáros saying that the measure of socialist progress is

the existence of substantive democracy at all levels of society.[25])
Finally, if there is a separate legal and administrative structure in
the state formations of all capital systems, the commune integrates
such structures and administrative practices into itself, restoring
the power of decision-making to the social body.

Overall, with Mészáros and Chávez, one can appreciate a
radical departure from most socialist prescriptions, both those
that have existed in the past and many of those still operating
in the present. In the past, socialists generally underestimated
the complexity of the transition and failed to perceive the central
importance of creating a new grassroots social metabolism. The
result was the persistence of the capital system in a hybrid form,
with the state and its functionaries taking over from individual
capitalists the role of extracting surplus labor from workers.
Today, many socialist projects continue to operate under the
assumption that they can proceed by simply obtaining political
power and offering a "better package" to workers and other sectors of society without much focus on workers' self-activity in
reshaping the structure of society and themselves in the process.
At best, workers' self-activity and self-realization are considered
merely accessory to the revolutionary process or assumed to be
relevant only at a later stage.

Yet these are dangerous ideas. If a socialist party takes power,
where are the new human beings with socialist consciousness
who will defend it, when push comes to shove with consolidated
capitalist interests, as happened not too long ago with the Syriza
government in Greece? What force can cause state power under
the new regime to gradually disappear, instead of consolidating
itself as a retrograde power that ultimately leads to capitalist restoration? If the self-determined activity of labor, made concrete
in some kind of community-based institution like the commune,
is not present from the beginning of the transformation process,
then these questions remain essentially unanswered.

As we have tried to show in the foregoing, the hypothesis
pursued by Chávez, under the influence of, on the one hand,

lived revolutionary experience in Venezuela and, on the other, Mészáros's innovative thinking, is radically different from most of what has been tried in the socialist playbook. This hypothesis maintains that workers' self-activity and self-determined labor should be central and express itself from the beginning of the revolutionary process, while also offering a novel political and economic institution for that activity to take place: the commune. Unlike most other frameworks for socialist construction, this one has not been defeated, though it has also only begun to be tested. The various communes that exist scattered throughout Venezuela in highly embattled situations are bold outposts for this project, deeply informed by an unflinching critique of past failures, while looking toward creating a better, humanly satisfying and sustainable future. The next chapter looks at three of these communes in eastern Venezuela, with very different degrees of development.

5

Three Communes in the East

The eastern coast of Venezuela, which connects with the Antillean archipelago, is the zone of the first European invasions into the region. Here Spanish settler colonists made initial advances from their Caribbean safe havens onto the mainland some five hundred years ago, only to be strongly rebuffed by Carib peoples. Later, the British intruded here too, occupying the island of Trinidad in 1797, while their burgeoning commercial interests crept upstream along the Orinoco River basin. These lands were also the base from which the final chapter in the Venezuelan independence struggle would be launched two hundred years ago, relying both on the participation of Indigenous peoples and on resources provided by the recently liberated Haiti. The upshot of this region's complex and combative history is that, even today, the territory is crisscrossed by diverse cultures and traditions and has varied geostrategic linkages: it forms a kind of palimpsest on which some of Venezuela's most glorious moments of anti-colonial resistance and rebellion are inscribed.

The story of eastern Venezuela's struggles, however, is far from over. The latest chapter in this rich history is being written by new generations of Venezuelans, who are committed to socialism and are attempting to restructure society through the communal model that former president Hugo Chávez promoted from 2009 forward as the path to the socialist future. To get to know the region's socialist communes, some of which are said to be very advanced, Cira Pascual Marquina and I embarked on a trip that took us first to coastal Barcelona, then to the lush Valle de Guanape, and finally to Cumanacoa, in the region's sizable hinterland. The aim of this investigation was to see what was being born in this diverse and varied territory, under what influences, and what all of it boded for the future.

LUISA CÁCERES COMMUNE IN BARCELONA

Shortly before we arrived to Barcelona, our first destination, a high-profile visitor had come to the area. This was the much-watched YouTuber Luis Arturo Villar ("Luisito Comunica"), who had come with his team, camera, and checkbook in hand to Barcelona's Lechería neighborhood. Lechería is one of the most privileged urban developments in the country, forming a kind of bubble for the super-rich, who often arrive in private airplanes to avoid the hoi polloi that might interfere with the good life they have between enjoying the tropical climate, perfect Caribbean beaches, and exquisite food. Luisito's aim in visiting the region was to buy a luxury apartment, taking advantage of the low real estate prices that resulted from the country's economic crisis. The young YouTuber recognized the problems that most Venezuelans experience in the U.S.-sanctioned country, such as the lack of electricity and scarcity of basic goods. However, he also told his audience that he likes to invest with a view to future profits, and the apartment's extremely low price made it a great deal. In the end, Luisito was so delighted with his new acquisition that he dedicated an entire video to celebrating the bonanza: a fully equipped beachside apartment he had obtained for almost nothing.

Yet the realities of working-class, revolutionary Venezuela were not far away. No one would imagine that at a short distance—albeit in a much poorer neighborhood—was one of Venezuela's most successful urban communes. This commune is called Luisa Cáceres de Arismendi, after a fourteen-year-old patriot who disarmed and shot her royalist captors in the struggle for independence two hundred years ago. Because the commune is inside Venezuela's sizable port city of Barcelona, the Luisa Cáceres initiative can be seen as a test case for urban communes. These present a unique set of problems for the communal movement. However, since most of the country's population lives in these zones, such problems cannot be ignored. Prominent among them is that all communes need to have a productive base, but what can an urban commune produce? A rural commune can grow food crops or raise cattle, an Andean one can cultivate coffee and cacao, a seaside commune can do fishing and fish processing. Yet urban areas, which are mostly residential in Venezuela, remain something of a riddle for the communal movement. For Luisito, the opportunity presented by an urban area fallen on hard times may have been clear: speculation on property values. But what can a socialist commune do in the concrete jungle of Venezuela's huge cities?

THE FIVE-HOUR DRIVE THAT takes Cira and me from Caracas to Barcelona, passing by Anzoátegui state's giant oil refining and shipping operations, goes quickly. When we arrive at the commune's headquarters, we encounter a half-acre walled lot with various shipping containers along its perimeter, as well as a garden and improvised gazebo. The communard who receives us, Carlos Herrera, sits us down in the gazebo and bluntly explains the dilemma of Venezuela's urban communes. "What grows here in these cities"—he pauses for effect—"are just shops and alienation!" Carlos briefly recounts the commune's six-year history, focusing on its various false starts in finding a viable economic project. Most of its initial efforts in developing productive

undertakings ran aground. However, the communards' stub-
bornness paid off when they finally discovered a solution,
which turned out to be as crude as it was obvious. The fact is
that all cities produce trash—and lots of it! So with a rebellious
spirit worthy of its pistol-slinging forebear, the Luisa Cáceres
Commune has tackled head-on the problem of having a source
of income in an urban area by taking over an important section of
the city of Barcelona's garbage collecting.

This was not the commune's first income-generating project.
Rather, it is one they arrived at after other experiments. An initial
project of the commune was processing corn flour, the primary
staple in Venezuela, used for making *arepas*, *hallacas*, *bollos*,
and *empanadas*. They obtained the machinery to grind and
package the product, and even attempted to go up the supply
chain by seizing land in the nearby township of Mallorquín
where the raw material, white corn, could be cultivated. Yet the
Luisa Cáceres communards found that, after a short time, they
could not compete with the producers in the private sector. "We
lost the battle to sell corn flour," Carlos says, "but in the process, we learned about supply chains and the need to plan our
undertakings." Luckily, another option emerged when the one-
time television reporter Luis Marcano, who was then mayor of
Barcelona, made good on a campaign promise that he was going
to transfer responsibility for city services to no fewer than nine
local communes, each of them charged with trash collection in
its respective area.

The communards at Luisa Cáceres seized upon this opportunity. Their doing so turned out to be fortunate for residents in the
zone, for as things played out, the other eight communes quickly
gave up the ghost. They were less aggressive, allowing the former
municipal truck drivers to continue working in trash collection, which led to conflicts, because these drivers were not fully
committed to the project. By contrast, the Luisa Cáceres communards understood—perhaps a lesson that they had learned
from their having half-control over the corn supplies: you must

control the entire chain—that having only partial responsibility
was dangerous territory. They insisted on running the whole
trash-collecting operation themselves, with their own drivers.
Whereas the other eight communes quickly saw their trash-collecting service fall apart with any minimal obstacle, this group
of communards was able to face and address obstacles as they
emerged, all in the spirit of cooperation. In effect, praxis makes
things perfect! By controlling the full process, the Luisa Cáceres
communards could make the corrections that were needed. They
could suffer the consequences of their own errors and enjoy the
benefits of their successes, doing so in a context of mutual respect
and recognition.

THE EXPERIENCE OF LUISA CÁCERES COMMUNE is a fascinating
example of how things can work efficiently in a social context
involving cooperation and mutuality in the workplace. To see
how it played in the community at large, I followed the commune's garbage truck, lovingly baptized *Lucho*, as it made its
rounds through the surrounding barrio. The whole process was
a relatively ludic and extravagantly social undertaking. With a
cluster of communards and neighbors crowded around it, the
commune's garbage truck advanced slowly through the working-class zone, with its low-lying houses and small shops. The
smell of ripe garbage notwithstanding, the entire operation had
the air of a church picnic. People came out of their houses to
talk with the drivers, since they are just as interested as the commune's workers in keeping the streets and city clean. Instead of
the conflict that is always present when capitalist management is
involved—an antagonism that affects both workers and clients—
there was cooperation, a good atmosphere, and a festive spirit.
Even the much-loved garbage truck was treated with affection
and respect. The truck had a name and was part of the family!

It is said that a "moral economy" is an essential part of working-
class consciousness. Instead of impersonal transactions based on

economic value—the rational calculations of an abstract *Homo economicus*—the working class applies notions of fairness, reciprocity, and equilibrium to exchanges and other interactions. For this reason, in spaces that workers themselves control, attitudes and behaviors based on solidarity come into play, while consensus-based norms and obligations often trump strict considerations of value, transcending the so-called cash nexus.[1] This is the positive side of a moral economy; its benefits, for a society and its members, are evident.

Yet any productive undertaking or service, even garbage collecting, requires resources. What is fair compensation for the services rendered? That is a question the Luisa Cáceres Commune had to face early on. Arriving at agreements with the neighbors was not an easy task, given that the ten years of oil bonanza had accustomed Venezuelans to free services and made "gifts from the government" into the baseline for fairness in society. Even so, the communards were able to make inroads into popular consciousness by using persuasion and through the example they set in ensuring a regular service of garbage collection. Often, they would approach the issue of compensation obliquely, simply asking people if they were satisfied with the service and what they thought it was worth. They also began to direct their minimal overhead to social services, such as a women's center and other projects benefiting their neighborhood.

All of this is part of the logic of a moral economy. A dense network of customs and traditions determines what is correct and acceptable, serving as a basis for appeals to a legitimacy that goes beyond mere legality. The communards at Luisa Cáceres have tried to work this angle. However, it goes with the territory of the moral economy—and this is the negative side of responding to such a moral polity—that they are sometimes accused of being merely a local mafia since they control resources that, despite social work and social outreach, are not yet under direct control of all members of the zone. Managing conflict and these kinds of contradictions in a socialist transition has become an important task for them. When you occupy or take charge of a public project, who will benefit initially? And how is this justified?

THESE PROBLEMS OF COMMUNITY relations came to a head with a second project of the commune, which is our next stop. That project is an occupied Mercal grocery store that is a short trek from the walled-lot headquarters where the commune's garbage collecting operation is based. The Luisa Cáceres communards took over the storefront space a few years ago because it was not delivering the subsidized food that is the basic remit of Mercal, a distribution project dating from the early years of the Bolivarian process. The spirit of emulation also played a role in the occupation. The Luisa Cáceres communards were in communication with comrades in El Maizal, perhaps the most advanced commune in Venezuela, which was boldly seizing land in Lara State on the other side of the country at about the same time. The communards here wanted to advance too in their own territory. They were also aware that the Mercal storefront, which had fallen on hard times during the blockade, was about to be privatized. It was the moment to act!

Since the store manager was a woman, the communards sent three women as a vanguard. Communal parliamentarian Ingrid Arcila, who is here in the storefront today, took part in the seizure. She explains how they went to the manager and said, "Good afternoon. Please give us the keys and your phone. This Mercal is now in the hands of the commune." Doing things in this gentle way—they eventually returned the manager's phone and allowed her to call her daughter—they wished to avoid projecting a bad image in the community. The manager understood that resisting the communal takeover was pointless. After the communards occupied the space, they cleaned it, gave it a fresh coat of paint, and repaired its refrigerators. Now the Luisa Cáceres-run Mercal offers bags of food to the community and maintains its facilities at a level it had never before enjoyed. The storefront is also a space for the community to meet and organize. Its walls are draped with complex charts related to food delivery and campaign mobilization in the zone.

The Luisa Cáceres Commune puts great emphasis on self-government. It is also among the most collectively organized communes and least prone to individualistic leadership of those we have visited in Venezuela. One of its spokespeople is Johan Tovar, who has taken time from caring for his nine-year-old to meet with us in the Mercal storefront this afternoon. We are interested in learning more about commune-building in this urban area where the relation with a complex state apparatus is particularly thorny, involving close contact with the city government and its authorities. This is no minor issue, since Venezuela's rentier state, as it developed during the twentieth century, has long been the focus of mass expectations due to its control of the oil wealth.[2] In responding to our questions about the relationship with state power, Johan tells us about Chávez's attempts to remake and rethink the Venezuelan state from above—but he puts even more emphasis on grassroots practice in negotiating this relation.

Johan tells us that the most important, experience-based lesson for the Luisa Cáceres communards has been their growing awareness of the effectiveness and importance of self-organization. This has been learned from both their failures and their successes, which seem to depend directly on the degree of autonomous organization they have achieved. As Johan puts it: "We discovered that communal organization is viable, and communes teach us that self-government and communal production is the way to get out of the current crisis. However, we still have a long way to go. Self-government cannot just be a matter of words; it cannot be always a precarious balancing act between popular power and institutions. Full autonomy of the processes is a must, otherwise we could become an institutional appendix."

In a country where the idea of the benefactor state has entered deeply into popular consciousness (so much so that Venezuelan anthropologist Fernando Coronil called it the "magical state"[3]) grassroots autonomy will always be hard won, and it will certainly be hotly contested during a socialist transition. However, Johan's defense of what he calls "full autonomy" as against the "precarious balancing act" of overdependence on state institutions resonates with the basic thesis of the communal path toward socialism and the reason it can succeed where earlier, more statist socialist projects failed. The key point is that the communal strategy can succeed because it is more internally coherent than the state socialist model applied in the USSR and the other Eastern Bloc countries in the twentieth century. Regarding the latter, István Mészáros once wrote that the Soviet system was like a person who falls because they try to sit between two stools. His idea was that "actually existing socialism" was an incoherent hybrid of two mutually hostile systems, but without the efficiency (or the rationality) of either one.[4]

Because of its composite nature, the Soviet system had problems with control of the work process. It could neither apply the imposed, external discipline of the capitalist overseer nor could it rely on that of true socialist self-government, that is, the internal discipline of self-managed workers. This explains much of what happened in these countries, where there was essentially a problem of *too little* (not *too much*) socialism. Workers were told that the property of the means of production belonged to the whole society, including them, but they did not have a decisive role in determining how to employ the machinery or how to dispose of the product. For that reason, Soviet workers considered the "socialist means of production" to be not fully theirs, but someone else's—or, most often, nobody's! Social property was established through legal decree, but it was not something real or truly felt. Stories about factory life in the USSR speak abundantly to this. There was an irrational use of resources, a host of bad labor practices (including purposeful waste), "storming" (last-minute drives to fulfill the plan), the hoarding of inputs, and, eventually, collapse.

The communards at Luisa Cáceres have seen something similar play out in Barcelona, where they found that the other communes, which had only partial control of the garbage removal project, essentially "fell between two stools." No one, neither the state functionaries nor the communards, took responsibility for the service. As had occurred in the Eastern Bloc, social property existed only on paper. The buck was continually passed, and the drivers eventually rebelled because they were not an integral part of the project. For these reasons, there is a continual push at Luisa Cáceres Commune toward more self-government and greater self-management in production. There is still much to be done, as the communards here are the first to admit. The most important thing, however, is that having chosen a coherent path they are avoiding the impasse of the earlier socialist model.

VISITING THE LUISA CÁCERES COMMUNE has been a learning experience because of the challenges that come from the urban context, including the proximity of state power. On our last day before leaving, we return to the walled-lot headquarters. It is midday and people are busy, sorting plastic material from the truck that has just come back from a morning round of garbage collection. We find ourselves examining a splendid mural on the commune's north wall that depicts the courageous patriot Luisa Cáceres herself, along with other Venezuelan notables. The young revolutionary appears here wearing a period dress alongside a rising sun and in the company of communist poet Aquiles Nazoa. This has become the commune's preferred space for group photos (not selfies!), and it is the symbolic and moral center of the commune. Standing before this mural, which connects the country's rebellious past with the communal future, it occurs to me how far this impressive commune is—in a social, rather than physical, sense—from the quotidian performance of individualism that most YouTubers, including Luisito Comunica, trade in.

When the communards notice our presence, they take a break

from sorting plastic to join us for photos in front of the mural. We take these pictures enthusiastically, as mementos, to eager shouts of "¡*Comuna o nada!*" Then, at the suggestion of communard Rosa Cáceres (no relation to the eponymous forebear on the mural), we devote some time to touring the commune's recycling operations—closely connected to the waste removal project that is their mainstay—and the community plant nursery they maintain. Urban gardening is something that became common in the Bolivarian Process, often inspired by Cuban "organoponic" methods. These Cuban gardens have been extremely successful in their home country and have helped overcome the island's legacy of monoculture. In his last years, Fidel Castro himself took much interest in these gardens and fervently promoted the cultivation of multi-use moringa trees there, said to be an excellent food source and have other health properties.

Here in this Venezuelan commune, urban ecology and conservation have been natural areas of work for the communards. They have found that simply by caring for urban spaces, they can preempt some of the sanitation problems in the city. For this reason, the communards use the plant nursery in this lot to cultivate ornamental flowers and bushes that they later place in spots that had formerly been used for dumping trash. Rosa tells us that the plants help people to see the city and its spaces as theirs and to attend to them spontaneously, on their own. "One of our objectives here is to change the 'chemistry' of sites that have become informal dumpsters," she says. The workers put the plants in strategic locations, often using old tires as planters, as they move around the city collecting garbage. The nursery also hosts edible plants and herbs. I ask about a moringa tree, wondering if the tidings of Fidel's pet project have gotten to this distant location. Rosa points to a scraggly but tall sapling, with numerous dangling seed pods—one of which I eagerly pocket.

Along with the plant nursery, the communards recycle both metal and plastic, providing an additional source of income. When the garbage truck *Lucho* arrives, the waste is carefully separated. Neighbors also bring bags of plastic bottles to the site. Recycling exists all around the world now, and the separation of waste has become a sort of global norm, with color-coded trash cans found in most major cities. However, the work in this commune has more social substance and economic importance than the recycling operations (or, for that matter, most community gardens) of the Global North. A visitor can see how the communards have adopted the globalized slogan, "Reduce, Reuse, Recycle," painting it on the commune's walls. The connection to a worldwide movement is likely meaningful for these communards. However, it is important to recognize that these terms mean something more substantial here. In the context of a Venezuelan commune—where *reducing* is imposed by the crisis and the blockade, *reusing* is a productive undertaking, and *recycling* an existential necessity—the slogan also goes hand in hand with new social relations.

It is meaningful, too, that their community garden bears the name of Pablo Characo, a longstanding opponent of transgenic seeds in Venezuela. Characo was an organic intellectual and supporter of the Bolivarian Process, who was born and lived not far from here. He died from COVID-19 last year but bequeathed to the country and region an autochthonous corn variant called Guanape MFE, which he preserved and promoted as an alternative to imported seeds. This lifetime project was carried out in the midst of a process of national liberation and social emancipation. In the context of this robust commune, it is gratifying to observe the workings of a grassroots and socially integrated ecology: environmental practices connected to the much-needed transformation of social relations that is required if ecology is to go beyond being merely symbolic activity and well-meaning gestures.

Monte Sinaí Commune in Valle de Guanape

Not all Venezuelan communes are success stories. It is part of

Venezuelan culture to suck in one's gut and hold one's head high in the face of adversity. Still, this heroic attitude can't disguise the serious problems that many communes in the country face today. In itself, the communal project is a simple one, far simpler than navigating capitalist market relations: in a communal situation, one produces to help oneself and help one's neighbors, with key decisions taken on the basis of people's needs and abilities. In fiction, it is common to represent scenarios of shipwreck and survival in these terms. Daniel Defoe's classic work *Robinson Crusoe* (1719) made its mark because of the relative isolation of its "army of one" protagonist, who became the model for *homo economicus* in much of classical economics.[5] However, this work is an exception. In most survival and shipwreck stories—for example, even the baby-boomer favorite *Gilligan's Island*—there is a varied group of individuals and a deliberative process takes place of assigning tasks according to abilities. Most likely, the popularity of survival fantasies is partly due to the attraction of their non-mercantile, more rational social relations. People find these situations interesting and meaningful, in contrast to the alienated labor relations they experience every day.

Despite the simplicity of communal relations, getting there—as with any promised land—can be hard. This is because one is "always already" organized by capitalist relations, and extricating oneself or others from them can be an act worthy of Houdini. Indeed, the task is even harder than that of an escape artist, since many of the traps and chains are internal ones. In the Monte Sinaí Commune in Valle de Guanape, these problems of inherited capitalist organization are experienced in many varied ways. One is geographical: the roads in the region keep people separated, in atomized groups, and this makes communal organizing more difficult, to say nothing of the complications their separation brings for sharing their production. Then there are the problems that come from Venezuela's being essentially an oil mono-producer, a situation that would not exist if it were not for capitalism's global market and the capital system's deep imbrication in fossil fuels.

Finally, there is the problem of ideology—the capitalist common sense that informs our daily thought processes and activities. Overcoming that ideological barrier is actually impossible in the short term—there are no magic bullets. Surmounting it is only viable through some iterative process involving self-activity and reflection.

At first, the Valle de Guanape zone, which has varied terrain and spreads across the states of Miranda and Anzoátegui, was organized as one huge commune. Yet this soon proved intractable, and it was broken into four smaller communes. Monte Sinaí, the commune we are visiting on our second stop, which we get to by backtracking from Barcelona toward Miranda State, most likely has its name because the majority of its members are evangelical Christians. Arguably, however, it would have been more accurate to name the commune Monte Ararat, since the communards here are essentially shipwrecked: the families live off subsistence agriculture and also produce some coffee and cacao as cash crops. Unfortunately, their cacao yields are minimal, and the coffee crop is in poor shape because their aging trees produce very little. The communards at Monte Sinaí know that to get things going, on the one hand, they have to improve the quality of the coffee trees, and, on the other, they need to begin to process (and thereby "add value to") the raw material produced in agriculture.

The commune is addressing the first problem, improving the quality of their crops, with its newly organized plant nursery. Here, with the support of the state-run Venezuelan Coffee Corporation, the Monte Sinaí communards are cultivating C27 seedlings, a new coffee variety that has greater productivity and pest-resistance. When our ride pulls into the abandoned city park where the nursery is located, we are received by Lenin González, a veteran worker associated with the commune. Seated near the stream that runs through the park, he explains the project's whys and wherefores: "Our objective now is to increase our production, which is very low now since most of the trees are old. Here, in Guacamayal Park, we have a nursery and we recently planted thirty-two kilos of C27 coffee seeds, which are sprouting right now." The commune has some 50,000 seedlings in the nursery, but the goal is to produce one million plants by 2023, which would fill Monte Sinaí's hills with coffee trees. This is no small project—it might be an economic game-changer for the commune—since a single hectare of C27 coffee can gross as much as $10,000 USD annually.

The effort to transform raw materials is being pursued in the family production unit, associated with Monte Sinaí Commune, which is the next site we visit. This is a cassava-wafer making project, where bitter yuca is transformed using thousand-year-old techniques. Not much has changed since pre-colonial times when Caribbean Indigenous people grated, strained, and toasted poisonous yuca to make these durable wafers. This was once done with slender baskets, stone-embedded wooden graters, and heated stone surfaces. The result was a non-perishable food that was an important staple developed by Arawak and Carib peoples, who used it as a food supply during long voyages. Today, all that has changed is a small diesel motor that drives a cassava grinder, and an aluminum *budare* griddle that has been substituted for a stone cooking surface. There is even a sad, scrawny donkey that brings the yuca to the site, an animal that looks like it has walked out of a colonial-epoch genre painting. Nothing could better illustrate the nature of the combined and uneven development that is typical of Latin America. Here in Venezuela a thousand-year-old process permits social reproduction—the reproduction of life—in a country whose principal commodity (literally) fuels advanced industrial production around the world.

Our last stop in this struggling commune involves attending a meeting of the Monte Sinaí communards in the village's public square. The gathering takes place in the shadow of a simple bust of Bolívar that presides over the square. One can easily observe how the speakers in this open space, even when talking about organizing the community and building socialism, make use of the inspirational style that is part of evangelical Christian culture. Communes and evangelical belief may seem like oil and water, but, in fact, great faith is needed to make a communal project go forward, that is, to project the communal "everything" out of the near "nothing" that these hopeful but destitute people live in. Speaking before those assembled is the gruff Alcadio Lemus, who is obviously the preacher in this community. He believes in the commune as much as he believes in his God. However, the project of emancipation that Alcadio is now promoting in this discourse, whatever its similarities to the spiritual one, has touched down on earth in this valley, and therefore involves both human and terrestrial emancipation. The words he uses to describe the goal are among the most purely revolutionary ones I have heard in some time: "We know that commune-building is a collective project: it's about the commons. As we understand it, a commune is about the *pueblo* organizing itself to produce and satisfy collective needs." Marx himself could hardly have said it better!

Cinco Fortalezas Commune in Cumanacoa

Eastern Venezuela is a world not only of abundant oil reserves and privileged beachgoers but also of sugarcane. The crop has long been grown in this region and forms an important part of the local diet both in its homemade varieties—brown-sugar loaves called *panela* or *papelón* along with fresh-squeezed *guarapo*—and in the pure crystalline form that results from industrial production. Even today, eastern Venezuelans are notorious for eating their black beans with sugar, which is heaped in generous spoonfuls onto the steaming plates of this staple food after serving. This odd practice—hot beans seasoned with pure sugar!—makes them the brunt of friendly ridicule from those who live in the center and west of the country.

Native to Oceania and East Asia, the sugarcane plant came to this zone in the hands of the colonists, who initially used the forced labor of enslaved people both to grow it and to carry out the extensive processing needed to turn the dark viscous liquid into pure white crystals. The market for sugar was huge, because European industrialization created a demand for a food that supplied quick energy to workers under the new discipline of the factory whistle. Sugar production soon became highly industrialized in the plantation economies of Venezuela and the rest of the Caribbean. The harsh, coercive, and debilitating labor conditions and concentration of workers led to forms of class struggle more akin to that of an industrial proletariat than typical rural confrontations.[6] The violence of capitalism, often hidden behind economic pressure in the Global North, bared its teeth and came out in the open in these plantations, where it provoked responses in kind. Sugar workers' struggles were explosive, far-sighted, and revolutionary. Cuban intellectual Fernando Ortiz, famous for his work on sugar and tobacco, commented on the rebelliousness and political clarity of sugarcane workers who "always have opposed interests to those of the owners and bosses," while poet and politician Aimé Césaire argued that Haiti's enslaved laborers in the sugar plantations— among the most glorious revolutionaries of all time—had acted like an industrial proletariat.[7]

Struggles over sugar production go on today, continuing this longstanding revolutionary tradition. In our trip through the eastern Venezuela region, our third and last stop takes us far inland to visit one of the most combative communes in the country. This is the Cinco Fortalezas Commune that was forged in the crucible of conflicts over sugar-producing lands and later a dispute with a sugar mill. Twenty years of the Bolivarian Process have done little to mitigate the violence surrounding capitalist sugar production in these parts. Speaking from experience, Yusmeli Dominguez, one of the commune's key leaders, tells us how her parents grew up in the perimeter of sugarcane fields where they worked as day laborers. "When I was a child, my parents had no land and they worked for the *terrateniente* [landowner]. We saw him getting richer and richer, while we had nothing. They gave him their lives, and he gave them nothing in return."

We are meeting in a patio of a former hacienda, taken over by the commune, which overlooks their collective sugarcane fields. Yusmeli tells us how roughly ten years ago people in the area began to occupy some abandoned fields and grow food crops there—this was the first step toward forming the Cinco Fortalezas Commune—but the sugar planters responded swiftly, cruelly destroying their crops. Even so, the people rallied and held onto the land, and a few years later they took over the sugar-producing lands of Hacienda Rosa, which became the commune's epicenter. These former day-laborers were fighting a battle on two fronts: they had the landlords on one side and the sluggish state on the other. Unfortunately, they had to struggle with the Venezuelan state because it colluded with the owners by dragging its feet in recognizing their right to the occupied land, despite how the communards' actions were backed up by the country's progressive 2001 Land Law.

The latest chapter in this struggle is a pitched battle with the manager of the region's state-owned sugar mill, Juan Ramírez, who in 2021 "bought" all the crops in the area, including those of the commune, but never paid for them. This scam, valued at some $300,000 USD, sent whole communities in the area spiraling downward and cost them many lives, particularly among the old and unwell, who could no longer buy medicines. The Cinco Fortalezas communards have appealed their case concerning the unpaid-for crops both to the state governor and the central government, but their complaints have gone unanswered. Their only option has been to carry out a "strike," refusing to harvest their sugar fields, which stretch out before us from our vantage point on the patio. At the same time, the communards are looking for other sugar processing options, including a nineteenth-century trapiche they have discovered nearby and hope to soon repair. Meanwhile, Juan Ramírez is refitting the sugar mill to process crude sugar from Argentina, as a way of turning his back on local growers entirely and making the state-owned mill independent of the country's endogenous production.

A BLOODY, NO-HOLDS barred battle of this kind requires enormous collective willpower and deep commitment. How else to survive the slings and arrows of capitalism's outrageous fortune? One of the things that most surprises me about this commune is the serene good humor of its militants and easygoing atmosphere they project in their speech and actions. It is marvelous how a dire situation and constant struggle have made them *more* and not *less* hospitable. Shortly after we arrive, the communards generously serve us lunch and converse with us over coffee and *guarapo*—the hot sun makes visiting the fields impossible at midday—but they are also eager to show us one of their "secret weapons" in the struggle against capitalism. This is the "mandala," a thatched hut structure they have built in the center of a circular herb garden.

The communards at Cinco Fortalezas describe their "mandala" as a space for reflection, meeting, and building community. Some aspects of the project can seem a bit hokey, since, for example, one enters the structure from one of four cardinal points depending on one's astrological sign. However, their "mandala" hut becomes quite a bit less contrived once you realize that every communal project needs a *symbolic* set of references of this kind. That is because all communes in Venezuela today are under construction and many features of communal work and life will necessarily be materially indistinguishable, for a while at least, from what one experiences and does in the non-communal world. Everything in these contexts is incomplete and in process. For this reason, only a discursive or symbolic register that expresses the *intention* of going in another direction—toward the goal of a communal society or socialism—can mark the commune's daily work as different, casting an alternative light on their activities and infusing a socialist spirit to practices such as tending a field or milking a cow, that are often materially identical to those one has always done.

Philosophers of mind have long pointed out how intentional states are notoriously inscrutable. How to discern the true motives of a person's actions? For Venezuela's commune builders, this is not a philosophical but a practical problem. It is the problem of how to create outward signs or marks, or what is sometimes called "*mística*" in Latin America's grassroots movements, to let everyone know that the arduous and often inglorious work of planting a field, harvesting a crop, milking cows, or tending to children, belongs to a shared project that is moving in an emancipatory direction. In Cinco Fortalezas Commune, this is done with the mandala; in El Maizal Commune there is the monument to Chávez and the nearby *caney* meeting space; in the Che Guevara Commune there are strategically located murals that adorn its concrete infrastructure; even the hard-hit communards in Monte Sinaí have their unique hybrid of evangelical faith and socialist science. Indeed, a quick review of the existing projects in Venezuela's communal movement reveals that most functional communes have something like this. Just as tellingly, it is the most problematic and precarious ones that lack a strong symbolic register.

When we are gathered in the mandala, seated on rocks around the hut's perimeter, we are told to let the overhanging thatch touch our hair. I am secretly hoping that this will be our last brush with anything approaching the esoteric. However, Yusmeli soon lets us have it with a blast of communard *mística*: "Everything from the rocks to the wood, to the plants that surround this mandala, comes from communal lands," she says to all those assembled. "The mandala's architectural form, with its four entrances, is loaded with symbolism: collective work, solidarity, and happiness. Chávez's spirit lives on here. We are his sons and his daughters, because we carry him in our hearts and in our consciousness." Despite my mistrust of such metaphysical language in other contexts, I can see how Yusmeli's discourse actually works in a very different, more practical register. Not only does it accompany real work and real struggle, but it also orients this project in a revolutionary direction.

Indeed, without such *mística*, all you would have in this commune, in strictly material terms, is the same person cutting cane, the same half-functional tractor, and the same scrawny dog as you had under capitalism. With mística, on the other hand, you can understand that the person cutting cane under the hot sun, the half-functional tractor, and the malnourished dog are all headed toward socialism! *Mística* marks daily activities with hopeful intentionality and a positive directionality. However, *mística* is only as good as the material reality it works to mediate. Surely because she is aware of this, Yusmeli next takes us abruptly back to earth to discuss the harsh social and political realities that these embattled communards are facing today. She does so without the faintest trace of otherworldliness: "We are still in a capitalist state that is guided by particular interests," she says. "In Venezuela, capitalism seems to have gotten control of the state and its institutions, and they don't believe in the bases."

IT IS FOUR O'CLOCK in the afternoon and the edge has been taken off the heat, so we head out into the fields amid the snaky sugarcane stalks. Now we are accompanied by communal leader Vanessa Pérez. Here in this commune all the main leadership roles are occupied by women. Vanessa, who has been involved in forming the Communard Union (see chapter 6), wants to tell us about their various projects, including fish farming and social work, and their plans for the future. Using a metaphor that has become common in Venezuela's popular movement, she says that sugar growing is this commune's "PDVSA." This figure of speech requires some unpacking. The idea is that, just as the profits from Venezuela's state oil company, PDVSA, were used by Chávez to diversify production and finance social projects, each commune should do the same on a micro scale, with some surplus-generating project financing its other activities. Hence "a PDVSA" refers to a goose that lays the golden eggs. It could be large-scale corn crops (as in El Maizal Commune), trash collection and recycling (as in Luisa Caceres Commune), or coffee and chocolate production (as in Che Guevara Commune), or something else depending on the region. In his discourses, Chávez often followed twentieth-century Venezuelan intellectual Arturo Uslar Pietri in referring to the reinvesting of oil profits as "sowing petroleum" (*sembrando petróleo*). Here in Cinco Fortelezas Commune the idea would be, though it is much less poetic, to diversify production and invest in the community by "sowing sugar."

Diversifying production and altering the productive apparatus is an urgent problem in the country, just as it is worldwide. Here in Venezuela the communal path toward socialism provides a theoretical template for this transformation. This is because an important part of communal life would be *communal consumption*, which involves adjusting consumption to people's true, more rational, and sustainable needs. Capitalism disconnects production and consumption—the two are separated by market mechanisms and the commodity fetish—but communes bring the two together and allow us to ask such questions as: Do people really need fossil fuels and sugar? And, if so, how much of them? For these issues to be resolved in a way that is not paternalistic or authoritarian, they must, of course, be sorted out democratically. Vanessa tells us about how in Cinco Fortalezas Commune they are trying to expand their projects—both in a productive and social sense—based on sugar profits: "The surplus produced by the sugarcane allows us to do work in the territory, from fixing the school or the roads, to public lighting, to getting medicine for those who need it, etc." It has also been used to start cultivating some food crops, such as peanuts, and to finance fish farming, which could be a good source of protein.

As our last stop, Vanessa takes us to look at some tilapia ponds where bright red fish swim in the shadow of the huge, bizarrely twisted cane stalks. These plants seem to have gone wild, like fairy-tale beanstalks, because they have been unharvested for so long. Looking at the fish, a small project embodying much hope for the future—all of which is surrounded by overgrown acres of a centuries-old plantation crop—I cannot help thinking about the complexity of the transition to communal socialism. The long-term aim may be clear, but the means for getting there are by no means simple, since almost surely continuing some level of sugar growing—and unfortunately some petroleum extraction—is needed in the immediate future before Venezuelans can abandon these problematic crops and resources and move toward something more humanly useful and sustainable. Purism is impossible here, if for no other reason than that, for the moment, the "badness" of sugar and the "evil" of petroleum are needed in this context to promote the "goodness" of something else.[8] Perhaps the mysticism of the nearby mandala has affected my brain, but I cannot help thinking how this represents a kind of socialist Catch-22 or is at least akin to Mészáros's puzzle of a house having to be rebuilt from within (see chapter 4). It is a difficult task, but not a thankless one. In the next chapter we will look at an important effort to address such problems of the socialist transition, by communes joining forces, pooling resources, and sharing information.

6

The Communard Union and Its Foundational Congress

Among the many challenges in rural organizing is a merely physical one: the distances that must be crossed. Producers in the countryside are, by the very nature of their work, separated across a territory and must come together to debate, socialize, and plan. In Venezuela, the problems endemic to rural organizing are heightened these days by the gas crisis and the scarcity of auto parts. This was evident one afternoon in early March 2022, when hundreds of people from around the country began to converge on El Maizal Commune in central western Lara State. They arrived in ramshackle buses, run-down trucks, and the occasional still-functioning personal car. They had endured hard travel conditions—heat, dust, and sometimes harassment by police officers asking for papers and more at roadblocks. Once on the grounds of El Maizal Commune, these committed people unloaded their sleeping bags and bedrolls, but they also unpacked banners, notebooks, and pamphlets. Who were these intrepid travelers and what drew them here? They were communard delegates from all around the country, hailing from most of the nation's twenty-three states, and they had come to El Maizal for three days of debate and planning.

As we have seen, communes became important during Hugo Chávez's last years when he developed a strategy of advancing toward socialism by using these grassroots spaces of self-managed production and substantive democracy as its basic cells. Since the president's untimely death in early 2013, the communal project he promoted has faced numerous challenges, including the rightward turn of his successor's government under the pressure of sanctions and hybrid war. Despite these challenges, commune-building goes forward in an almost miraculous way in the country, driven by grassroots forces whose commitment can be explained by a combination of loyalty to the former president, the pressing necessity to produce food, and their political consciousness. However, these communes, which are sown across the country and without much support, are embattled outposts, weakened by their isolation. This means that they have been forced by the overall capitalist context to make many concessions, especially in terms of commodity production. To begin to overcome this situation of isolation, there have been attempts to build unity among the country's communes. The most important of these is the Communard Union (*Unión Comunera*) whose Foundational Congress was the destination of the delegates arriving in buses, trucks, and cars to El Maizal in the dry heat of that March afternoon.

ORIGINS OF THE COMMUNARD UNION

Why build a league or union of communes? It is obvious that unifying and coordinating the work of these scattered projects is important if Venezuelan communes are not to be merely picturesque refuges but rather a counter-hegemonic system that reaches beyond the local to the national level and even beyond. The complication is that this coalescing force should come from below, from the grassroots, yet it must supersede the local. In effect, each space wrested from capital's logic is a battle won, but unless these diverse spaces collectively point to a widening sphere of emancipated territory—that is, unless there are advances on micro and macro levels at the same time—then such precarious first steps can easily be reabsorbed into capital's logic and its hydra-headed institutions. It is almost certainly for this reason that, in *Aló Presidente Teórico No. 1*, Chávez went so far as to say that an isolated commune is actually counter-revolutionary: "Communes are like cells, and cells have to go on branching out, forging connections," he said in that historic television program. "They have to create a system, link-up, to give shape to a body."[1] Clearly, then, the late president saw communes as part of an organic whole and future national system. Notably, too, the Communal Laws that were developed in 2010 as part of the package of five *Popular Power Laws*, propose associating the communes in communal cities, in federations, and also as the basis of a future "communal state."

All this is on the level of theory and legislation. However, the idea for a Communard Union, like most concrete steps in the communal movement, was in fact born under the pressure of necessity. The need for "a unifying and integrating instrument," as the Union describes itself in its statutes, emerged in great measure because the more advanced communes in the country found themselves alone in an adverse situation, marked by political regression and pragmatism on the part of the new governmental leadership.[2] For example, at El Maizal, possibly the most advanced commune in the country, people felt that they were facing both an external counterrevolution and what they call the internal, reformist "fifth column." Both the local bourgeoisie and the regional authorities were treating El Maizal Commune badly, while the government seemed to have turned its back on the project. Its charismatic leader, Ángel Prado, had even had an election for mayor taken away from him a few years back for bureaucratic reasons. The commune seemed to be cornered. For this reason, the communards from El Maizal felt the pressing need to build a network of support with other communes and other Chavista groups in the country.

There was a meeting, with the participation of ten communes, in Che Guevara Commune in Mérida in 2019. Here the first plans for the future Communard Union were laid. Then there were local meetings, five in total, for each of the country's major regions, while the promoting committee formed the Argelia Laya Brigade.[3] This was made up of youths who traveled the country under difficult conditions, connecting with incipient or abandoned communes and motivating their members. An important preliminary meeting took place at the Alí Primera Commune in Urachiche in 2021. The preparatory work of building the Union went on for almost three years, briefly interrupted by the COVID-19 pandemic. Along the way, the organizers were successful in generating interest and they made important steps toward reaching consensus. However, bringing the communes together into a nationwide movement necessarily evokes a host of questions about forms of leadership, decision-making methods, and critically, the relation of the communes to each other and of their Union to the state's institutions. Will this latter be a friendly relation, an antagonistic one, or a bit of both? Will the Union extend and develop the democratic principles that operate inside the diverse communes that make it up, presumably in a prefigurative mode? These were the burning questions that would have to be resolved downstream in the Communard Union's Foundational Congress.

THE DEBATES

Debates on these issues surfaced quickly in the Foundational Congress, which so many people had crossed the country in March of 2022 to attend, using whatever means of transport were available in the besieged country. Once these two hundred or so delegates from roughly fifty communes had dusted themselves off, recuperated from the trip with water and snacks, and plopped themselves into the neatly organized rows of seats arranged in El Maizal's machinery shed, the controversies and discussions began. Despite a good-natured, even festive atmosphere in the meetings, the delegates freely offered their opinions about diverse issues that the new Union would face. The question of state power and the relation of the Union to it was never far from the surface. For example, Ángel Prado, whose commune was hosting the event, told those assembled that he thought the fledgling Union should be committed to being just as *constructive* as it was *critical* in relation to the central government. To the degree that the communes criticize the state, they would also try to build something new and construct an alternative. Instead of antagonism with the state, Prado argued that what is really at stake were simply different visions of the country. "The government has its plan, its interpretation of the *Plan de la Patria* [the Plan for the Nation that Chávez developed]," he said, "while we have our own interpretation of the Plan!" Prado also pointed to the importance of supporting the government and its PSUV party in upcoming elections.

As the charismatic leader of a powerful rural commune, Prado has great moral authority. One might have thought that his position would set the tone for the remaining interventions. However, some other delegates tried to push the envelope of radicalness and put alternative visions on the table during the initial debates. For example, Johan Tovar from the Luisa Cáceres Commune in Anzoátegui State was clearly not so interested as Prado in supporting the ruling party as its rearguard. He said he wanted to see a "communal republic" emerge in Venezuela. Even more critical was Martha Lía Grajales from the San Augustín Convive initiative in Caracas, who went so far as to say that the government does not represent the people: it does not call on them to participate anymore. In the view of Grajales, who has had to confront state repression in the poor urban communities where she works, this made the Communard Union all the more important since the diverse self-organized groups around the country, much more than the state, were what was now maintaining Chávez's ideals and goals alive.

Among these varied perspectives—some more hopeful with regard to the state, others more pessimistic—one can perceive some of the fissures in the shifting sands of Venezuela's popular movement today. What is the relation of the movement to the government? Is it symbiotic, a kind of détente, or antagonistic? Should the communal movement aspire to replace existing state power and, if so, over what time frame? These questions are difficult and hard to get to the bottom of. An ambivalent relation to the state has long been a part of the political culture of Venezuela's social movements, where a loose, open-ended, and generally affirmative approach to state institutions predates the Bolivarian Process. Such practices were promoted and consolidated during the populist governments of the Fourth Republic (1958-98), but they were also reinforced during the two decades of Chavismo. This means that when Venezuela's social movements face state power today, there are almost no red lines, but rather a push and pull that depends on the circumstances.

THE MINISTER ARRIVES

The lack of red lines, and the full spectrum of behaviors associated with it, was on display after an important representative of the state itself arrived at the meeting. This was Jorge Arreaza, the new Minister of Communes, who pulled in at the head of his three-car entourage on the second day of the Congress. The minister's surprise visit elicited many echoes of Fourth Republic politics and its chummy populism. Arreaza was offered the microphone and he went before the audience, seemingly protecting himself with the red "Commune or Nothing!" T-shirt he was wearing and a recently gifted El Maizal cap pushed down over his head. There Arreaza gave a longish but humble discourse—wise ministers know how to adapt their words to different contexts!—the essence of which was that the ministry had few resources to help and that willpower, meaning everybody pitching in, would be key to the communal movement advancing. Overall, his words met with a generous and friendly reception. While there was some joking on the part of communard leaders about the ministry and its sometimes tense relation with communes, Arreaza's discourse met with hearty applause, and many audience members came forward to take selfies with the minister.

Arreaza was Chávez's son-in-law, and he has the reputation of being a reasonable person, more accessible than most bureaucrats, and a good listener. He had recently been working closely with grassroots forces during a campaign for governor in Barinas State where he tried to break the control of the corrupt branches of Chávez's family over that region. All of this may have helped tip the scales in Arreaza's favor. In fact, it is most likely that he was chosen by higher-ups as minister precisely because of his personal qualities and current street cred. The enthusiasm of people in the communal movement is understandable. Still, I learned from side conversations with some participants in the congress that they felt the incipient Communard Union's excess of flexibility and its tendency to improvise the relationship with state functionaries could spell future problems for the communal movement. Attempts to dance with the bureaucracy without any clear red lines usually end with the latter controlling and subordinating the popular movement and its projects.

The Program

Without doubt, these skeptics have Venezuela's history on their side. Similar movements in the recent past have generally run aground for this reason. One only has to look at what happened to the *Ezequiel Zamora Revolutionary Current*, a campesino movement born in 2005; *Chavismo Bravío*, an attempt to regroup the Chavista left around 2012–13; and the *Marcha Campesina*, which emerged in 2018. These movements and projects, each powerful in its time, have all become co-opted in one way or another, some even becoming appendices of the state and its official PSUV party. This meant that, as the Foundational Congress was packing up on the third day, having ratified the Communard Union's statutes and program and elected people to its different national and regional positions, there was much hope but also an understandable concern about the dangers of historical replay and appropriation. Debates and differences had emerged, and despite a strong commitment to not have them forcibly suppressed nor let them irreparably divide its ranks, there were still latent disagreements. The path forward, if admirably sketched out and ratified by the congress, would be by no means easy.

The Program and Statutes of the Communard Union that they had approved is a concise, nicely designed document. It is remarkably solid and constitutes a real asset, even a road map charting a way forward. The document's solidity in theoretical terms is hardly surprising, since it was drafted beforehand by the most radical and formed elements of the Communard Union. This is evident in both the program's language and its advanced contents. One key component is the centrality of popular power and substantive democracy. This is the Union's key programmatic element, which it combines with environmentalism, anti-imperialism, feminism, and socialism. The document's preamble takes a historical approach to explaining the country's communal project, charting the importance of grassroots democracy in the first decades of the Bolivarian Process. Through this historical recap, one can see how Chávez and the Bolivarian movement considered elections to be one thing—he called them "festivals of political machinery," even if he knew how to win them—but the Bolivarian proposal is really based on *participative and protagonistic democracy*. This was the revolution's real trump card, its essence, and the communal project grows out of that essence, the program says. The commune is the maximum expression of popular power and substantive democracy. Hence, the Communard Union is meant to continue developing these principles and ultimately work toward the elimination of the bourgeois state.

Based on this reading of recent Chavista history, in which

popular power is the guiding principle and driving force, the program affirms that the fundamental premise of the communal project is "participative and protagonistic democracy." However, it sees this as a dynamic, not static, principle, for at the same time it ratifies the importance of the communes as an emergent self-government, one capable of overcoming localism and later leading to the withering of the bourgeois state. This will be achieved through the subsequent forming of a Federation of Communes and finally the Communal State. The document also gives importance to socialist "formation" (that is, education), and it defends the principles of environmentalism, anti-imperialism, feminism, and gender diversity. The section on patriarchy and communal feminism calls for a class-conscious feminism and an end to the double exploitation of women. In economic terms, the Union's program stresses production under new social relations: it defends social property and production aimed at satisfying the community's needs. In general terms, the program commits to strengthening the communes' productive power, and, more concretely, to developing non-market distribution networks, called the "Sistema Nacional de Economía y Producción Comunal," among communes and other kindred organizations.

Overall, the Union's program reflects advanced, ambitious positions on key issues of the socialist transition. However, despite its sophistication, the program leaves open many questions related to the material and human means for carrying that strategy forward when the hard work of organizing, linking communes, and sharing goods and resources sets in. In that sense, some key issues are: When the Union tries to go forward over the next few years, will it be possible to conjugate the vanguard aspirations of the organizers with the interests of the bases? Will its commitment to communal feminism and gender diversity be cashed out in concrete transformations, such as achieving gender parity and non-binary inclusion in leadership positions inside the Union and in the communes that make it up? Will the Union maintain its principles, and strategy, which are solidly socialist, in the face of state actors? Perhaps most important is the question of whether the Union could become the lever that rejuvenates the Chavista movement as a whole, restoring its earlier commitment to socialist emancipation via the commune.

CHALLENGES AND SOLUTIONS

We have mentioned that rural organizing is difficult in any circumstance. The localist cosmovision of many rural producers and their physical separation are notorious challenges for all such organizations worldwide. However, the truth is that any national-level popular organization, not just a rural one, is hard to construct in Venezuela. This is because the country's formal working class is small, and the productive apparatus, based essentially on oil extraction and refining, is largely confined to relatively small enclaves. That means most of the population lives in something like what has historically been the atomized peasant condition, even in cities, and it is difficult to build an organization that is bigger than six to eight people—the size of a group of friends or a large family.

In this peculiar situation, one of the few national organizations in Venezuela, an organization that reaches over the whole territory, is the country's military. It is the military's territorial reach, far more than its possession of arms, that makes the institution so important in the Caribbean nation, and its importance is above all political rather than military in a strict sense. The armed forces' territorial reach, along with its surprising class character, explains why Venezuelans have often turned to the military to carry out political tasks. Meanwhile, civilian organizations, even left ones, scramble to bring together workers and citizens despite the lack of workplace connections and the cultural challenges that they must grapple with when it comes to forming unions. Quite often these left organizations become pragmatic and adopt similarly hierarchical, centralist methods. In fact, the country's longstanding practice in political and social contexts, even grassroots ones, is to insist that there be widespread democracy and a certain level of horizontality (these are also part of the political tradition) while simultaneously injecting strong doses of top-down centralism to avoid chaos and increase their organizations' effectiveness.

Some of this organizational culture has affected the Communard Union, its methods, and its relation to its bases. It will also inevitably inform its efforts to expand and promote the unity of communes over the upcoming years. True to historical pattern in Venezuela, the Union, even if it is firmly committed to democratic participation, still has opted to give great power to a central committee and its cadres. This is the tried-and-true historical formula in Venezuela. There is a national direction to the Union and also regional directions in each of the Plains, Andes, Central, Center West, and Oriental regions. Both national and regional leaders will meet with some frequency, but the meeting of the whole organization will happen only once every four years. This makes for a strong centralized apparatus that, even if it *reaches out* to the bases, nevertheless falls short of *incorporating* them into daily decision-making and governance. Moreover, as an internal mode of decision-making, the Union has opted for "democratic centralism." This is a wonderful organizational principle, yet it has historically been much more *centralist* than *democratic*. Among the unfortunate consequences of the centralist and hierarchical structure of the organization, partly imposed by lack of resources, is that the bases, since they do not see themselves eye-to-eye as much as they see the leaders, will almost surely begin to perceive the leadership as a power apart or even a conduit to the state.

MATERIAL AND GLOBAL REALITIES

These were some of the outstanding issues when the Communard Union's Foundational Congress came to a close and the delegates packed up and took their leave of each other, with a deserved feeling that they had taken part in a historic triumph for the country's communal movement. However, in the summer and fall after the congress took place, when I checked back on friends working in the Communard Union, I learned that they had indeed faced many problems in bringing the Union's ambitious program to fruition. The Union had been working on food distribution projects (called *rutas*), to encourage non-market exchanges of fish, meat, cheese, and coffee among communes and also to bring rural food production to Caracas. The aim of this project was to break the hold of capitalist intermediaries between rural production and urban consumption. Still, none of the *rutas* had actually been initiated; the logistical problems had proven overwhelming. The Union was too short on resources to kick-start the distribution processes, and it had made almost no advances on the economic front in five months. Even so, they had done work in other areas. For example, the Union had successfully organized some events, including one hosted by Tatuy TV, to educate militants in communication techniques, and another involving leadership training. They had reactivated the Argelia Laya brigade, and had managed to consolidate the participation of some Plains region communes into the Union even if the country's most important urban commune, El Panal, still remains outside.

The stories from my contacts in the Union all spoke for its members' strong commitment, as shown in its impressive deployment of cadres throughout the country, but there were also serious obstacles, quite often related to the situation of the neediest communes and the expectations of the Union's bases. One Union cadre, who had gone on some of these trips, remarked on how the immediate aim of those in most communes around the country rarely goes beyond getting financial or material support. Moreover, as could be anticipated due to the Union's structure, the majority of communes look to it simply as a communication channel with the state. Indeed, the Union's hierarchical structure tends to relegate the grassroots to pursuing corporative, sectoral interests over the political project, while the leadership finds itself somewhat isolated in pursuing its more ambitious goals of forcing the hand of the state and hegemonizing the country. This situation suits the state and the ministries well, since they prefer to deal with communes either one by one or as part of networks that they manage themselves, as is evidenced in the Ministry of Commune's recent launching of a "communal circuit" project, that in some ways rivals the Union's self-organized *rutas*.[4]

In evaluating organizations, it is always important to look closely, beyond their explicitly conceived aims, at their position within the framework of the country's economic activity. What is the economic basis of the Communard Union, and its relation to other economic actors in the country? This is the Ariadne's thread that runs through many organizational projects, and it can help us understand the real forces that they deploy and with which they must engage. Sometimes such material issues have almost as much impact as what is said or has been committed to paper. In a Venezuela that is under a cruel U.S. blockade, material resources are extremely scarce, with most people living very little above the survival level. The same could be said for the struggling organizations that might enter the Communard Union. Most of them must operate more as potential beneficiaries and very little as potential donors. That means that they might subscribe to the Union and even endorse its combative spirit and political program, but they have neither the resources nor necessarily even the will to engage in a war of positions with the power of capital or the state, which has historically been the financial basis of even grassroots organizations in the country.

The Venezuelan communes and their new unifying organ, the Communard Union, are hopeful players in this context, but they are not free from its complexities and contradictions. As far as the Union's staying power is concerned, it has as assets the strength of some very powerful communes on its side, as well as the legacy of grassroots Chavismo's long trajectory of struggle. Moreover, despite the challenges related to its limited internal democracy and its residual hierarchies, it is also possible that these problems are as much *effects* as *causes* of the Union's weakness. That means that the gradual accumulation of forces, especially if there are similar advances in the rest of the Latin American region, could tip the scales in favor of the Union and Venezuela's communal movement more broadly, as they advance. There is cause for optimism on this front, for a brief survey of the region, and even the world today, indicates that there are many kindred progressive movements emerging in our time, the convergence of which could be important as the Communard Union attempts to carry forward Chávez's historic project in the face of future challenges. The next chapter looks at how a group of industrial workers in Venezuela is engaging with the communal movement.

7

The Guayana Region: Communal Practices and Solidarity Brigades among Industrial Workers

Much ink has been spilled on the question of why Latin American countries cannot industrialize, with economies that generate long-term, self-reinforcing backward and forward linkages. Indeed, recent history speaks clearly for what seem to be the Sisyphean challenges of development in the region. Instead of independent industrialization and autonomous growth, Latin American countries have tended, almost inexorably, to play the role of junior partners that depend on the Global North's economies, which determine what and how they will produce. This happens, moreover, in a way that benefits not their own development but the North's. Because it is so persistent, the region's economic dependency can seem almost like a destiny, an evil star under which Latin American countries were born that makes most of the profits and value they generate slip through their fingers, only to mysteriously reappear in the ledger books of U.S. and European multinationals. It is true that Brazil, Mexico, and Argentina all underwent limited processes of industrialization in the mid-twentieth century. However, before that century ended, those hopeful national economies saw their

fledgling industries cut back and their roles as dependent export-
ers of raw materials affirmed. As before, the rich countries went
on getting richer and the poor countries relatively poorer, while
South-to-North value transfer continued unabated.

Why can't Latin American countries develop along lines they
themselves generate independently? German-American economist Andre Gunder Frank was able to tear away many ideological
veils that cover the issue of dependency, with an approach that
looked at the world system as a structured organic totality. That
perspective allowed him to refute the idea that capitalist development, wherever it takes place, is necessarily progressive. That
might be the ideology we all receive, but for many countries, as
Frank aptly pointed out, their position in the world system determines that their "development *is* underdevelopment." In keeping
with this holistic approach, Frank and his fellow dependency theorists understood that the logic of capital, when operating on a
global scale, like capitalism inside a given nation, generates poles
of development and underdevelopment, or the "simultaneous
generation of development in some parts and underdevelopment
in others."[1] This implies that not all boats of the world's nations
can be lifted with "the rising tide," as Adam Smith once optimistically suggested, but rather the rising of some nations depends
on the sinking and subordination of others. The capitalist world
system is thus by nature an unequal playing field. Once it is set
in place, countries will enter as either central (core) or peripheral (dependent) nations. If a new player somehow manages to
become a dominant or central country—as South Korea did,
through a process begun in the 1960s—it will be the result of a
reshuffling that guarantees that other countries and other peoples
become *its* periphery, from which value can in turn be drained.[2]

THE BASIC INDUSTRIES OF GUAYANA

These reflections on dependency and value transfer can seem
very abstract, as indeed any high-level schema concerning

the nature of the capitalist world system will be. However, in Venezuela's Guayana region, which Cira Pascual and I are visiting as part of our investigation into grassroots movements and communal projects, dependency is not a mere abstraction but rather a material, visible reality. Here one can see the limits of dependent industrialization spelled out in concrete facts, precisely because the Guayana region is the site of a huge, planned effort at industrial development that got going with the inauguration of the hydroelectric projects on the Caroní River around 1960. The energy, the resources, and the technology were all dutifully secured and put in place. Yet somehow the goal of autonomous development remained elusive, even chimerical. This colossal effort, involving tens of thousands of workers and massive capital investments, may have led to some level of industrialization and reflected significant political will. However, as if some Greek oracle had spoken, this immense project turned out to be yet another expression of Venezuelan dependency. The new industry was not so much *value-capturing* as *value-draining*, in a further iteration of the dynamics of the unequal world system.

When you drive toward the Guayanese industrial zone from the major city of Puerto Ordaz, you follow the twisting Orinoco River with its beige silt-laden waters. The route passes by one gargantuan skeletal structure after another. Because of the deteriorated, abandoned state of these factories, it is an almost post-apocalyptic scene that emerges before your eyes. What you are witnessing are the so-called basic industries of Guayana, which do the first stages of iron, aluminum, and now gold processing. The first step in building the industrial complex of Guayana goes far back. In the 1950s, under the dictatorship of Marcos Pérez Jiménez, a small steel plant called Sivensa was built. However, it had also been determined that the huge amounts of relatively silt-free water flowing from the region's Caroní River constituted perfect conditions for building hydroelectric plants that could fuel a wider range of energy-intensive industries. A series of dams, including the flagship Guri project, which generates 11,000 megawatts a day, were built in the 1960s, along with the Sidor steel plant and a pair of state-of-the-art aluminum plants. They were all expanded during the 1970s oil boom. The business model applied in this enclave was simple and efficient, triangulated as it was between almost free energy, cheap labor, and copious raw materials. Moreover, the semi-processed output generated by these industries could often simply be rolled downhill on narrow-gauge railways, then into waiting ships on their way to the Global North. As we have indicated, the destiny of the country's dependency could not be undone by the project, despite its scale and the resources invested in it. All this effort simply repeated the process of bleeding out that Uruguayan writer Eduardo Galeano referred to when he wrote about the "open veins of Latin America." Economic value still flowed out of the region like blood, feeding the vampire of the North's industry and *its* development.[3]

In Venezuela, political regimes of all colors have attempted to overcome this subordinate condition. The dictator, the liberals, the Christian democrats, and even Hugo Chávez tried their hand at breaking the spell of dependency that hangs over the Guayana industrial complex. Yet neither nationalization, mixed industries, privatizations, nor plans to diversify could overcome the dependent condition and produce the desired results. Independent development remained relentlessly elusive, and the new industries continued as mere appendices of capital accumulation elsewhere. The rusting structures in this industrial wasteland, some sixty years after the project got going, and the many unemployed or underemployed workers that populate the region, are eloquent evidence of this. But now there is a new way of working that is emerging from a handful of self-managed and occupied workshops in the zone, which may constitute the light at the end of the tunnel as far as dependency is concerned.

This new modus operandi coming from the grassroots could be the game-changer that Venezuelan people have been waiting for—and an example for other countries in the region. It represents a radical move away from the longstanding practice of just generating commodities for an anonymous international market—whose value seems to always slip away along the world's value chains—toward doing work for specific communities and with their explicit needs in view. Moreover, inside the self-managed workshops that a set of ambitious and politically conscious workers have occupied in Guayana, most of them shops that serve the metal industry, new practices involving solidarity, voluntary labor, and use-value production are now in center stage instead of on the margins of the production process. This embodies the spirit or perspective of the commune, and it is interesting to see how communal values play out in the industrial setting of these metallurgy workshops.

All of this has whetted our curiosity about the Guayanese industrial zone, and helped us to understand that though there may be few *de jure* working communes in this region of Venezuela, there are nevertheless emergent practices that respond to the same values, essential social relations, and guiding principles that underpin the communal movement elsewhere in the country. Importantly, the values of solidarity and mutuality not only orient production inside the occupied, self-managed workshops, but they have also driven the most politically conscious workers to apply their skills as qualified technicians to help jump-start production in different grassroots projects all across the country, including communes. With time, they have formalized this ambitious practice of sending solidarity brigades around the country, calling it the *Productive Workers Army*. Overall, one senses that the new approach expressed both in these self-managed shop floors and in the Productive Workers Army could be an initial step toward finally dispelling the specter of dependency in Venezuela, but this time by framing development as something close to the ground that is shaped by people's real needs and goals as self-determined agents. Or at least that is the bright promise—a promise that has both social and ecological dimensions—held out by the new, more "communal" practices of production that are taking shape in Guayana these days. The stories we have heard about these projects in the region have inspired Cira and me to make the almost 500-mile trip from Caracas to investigate its self-managed workshops.

Occupying Indorca

The epicenter of these emergent practices is composed of mid-size worker-controlled ateliers that serve Guayana's basic industries. Foremost among them is Industrias del Orinoco, or *Indorca*, a metallurgy workshop whose niche is precision machined parts and repairs for the steel industry. Indorca had been a private business until ten years ago. However, repeating a pattern that has occurred throughout the zone, its owner began to shut down the plant in response to the new progressive labor law, the LOTTT, that the Bolivarian government passed in 2012 to give workers more rights. Since Indorca's owner had been reducing hands on the shop floor and removing equipment for some time, the workers had seen the writing on the wall and begun to prepare. This meant that when the shutdown eventually occurred, they were ready to act. They seized Indorca's installations, put a heavy chain around the outside gate, and slept by turns on site for two years to keep the owner from retaking control or sabotaging the business. Occupying the plant was a bonding experience that stuck with Indorca's staff and transformed their political consciousness.

The story of the occupation of this metallurgy workshop, undertaken when Venezuela was just on the brink of its economic crisis, is rich with anecdotes that still circulate among its workers. After our taxi drive from Puerto Ordaz to the Indorca plant, we first tour the hangars where the enterprise's heavy machinery, including lathes and welding equipment, now operate. What we encounter inside these structures is a scene of impressive peace and order: fifty or so staff members working diligently and harmoniously in a remarkably non-antagonistic

context. The operations seem efficient, smooth, and the atmosphere among workers amenable. However, the workers we talk
to in the plant are eager to tell us that this radically changed environment is hard-won, the result of intense struggle. For example,
when Indorca's workers originally seized the plant, putting the
chain on the gate, they could not even get inside. This meant
that they had to sleep by turns in an open, thatched structure
called a *maloca* by the entrance, fending off repeated attacks by
the owner's goons and the police. They did this for two long
years, showing impressive resilience and resourcefulness. Since
this was a time when severe shortages of basic goods were beginning to affect the country, they had to supplement their food with
iguanas and plantains they scavenged nearby. One worker, nicknamed "the Wizard," tells us how a group of the owner's hired
goons assaulted and bound him one night when he was cooking *cachapa* corn pancakes on an open fire. The armed band not
only robbed the workshops, taking away machinery and electric
cables, but added insult to injury by eating the corn pancakes in
front of the Wizard who had been turned into a hogtied spectator
at his own dinner table!

During this extended vigil outside the factory, a small group
of Indorca workers traveled to Caracas to make their case for
self-management before the government, based on Article 149
of the LOTTT, which makes occupying an idle factory legal. As
workers from the interior, they had few contacts in the capital
city, so they had no choice but to sleep in the streets, covering
themselves with cardboard while living off white bread and cola
drinks that they bought from streetside cafes. Eventually, the
determined workers got an audience, not with Chávez, as they
had hoped, but with a sympathetic military officer from his personal staff who put them in contact with the Minister of Labor.
This is how Indorca got recognized as a legal factory occupation.
Then, to get the business going again, they had to appeal to active
workers in the zone who pitched in by bringing their know-how
and replacement parts for the missing machinery and cables to

Indorca. This help came mostly from the nearby self-managed workshops Equipetrol and Calderys, also in the Guayana zone, with the neighboring workers giving their abundant support voluntarily. The Indorca workers also implemented a radical form of horizontal democracy internally, along with equal pay for all workers and transparent bookkeeping.

In this whirlwind of support and solidarity, in what was essentially a community barn-raising effort, Indorca's workers now began to look outside the confines of their own business. The experience of sharing that was born during the occupation process—especially the long days and nights spent in the *maloca*—and the help from other workshops had transformed Indorca's workers profoundly, endowing them with a communal perspective. In the spirit of reciprocity, they now thought: *We have received a lot of help, now who needs our help?* José "Cheo" Cedeño, a skilled machinist and the charismatic leader of Indorca's workers, remembers that period as a difficult but beautiful time. He recalls: "We were without jobs, but worker solidarity kept us alive, and we began to think about our potential as a class. We realized that while we have no money, together we have a lot of acquired knowledge. Let's jump-start a few factories together!" This was the germ of the idea of what later became their solidarity brigades, or the Productive Workers Army.

As luck would have it, a union leader from a state-owned sardine-processing plant in the coastal city of Cumaná soon got in touch with the workers at Indorca, asking for help with their broken canning machinery. This was just the opportunity to express solidarity that Indorca's workers had been waiting for, and they prepared a volunteer brigade for the coast. Cedeño, who is normally very serious and understated, brightens up when he tells us how this solidarity project got going. His story about how their brigade saved the sardine plant takes us beyond the daily routine of work on the Indorca shop floor to a narrative register that involves adventure, sacrifice, and high ideals. The La Gaviota sardine-processing plant had been on hold for months, mostly because their oven for preparing fishmeal was broken. The workers there did not know much about industrial equipment and repairs. Cedeño tells us that, after making a preliminary diagnosis of their problems, he gathered skilled workers and supplies from the Guayana region, incorporating volunteers from the two other nearby self-managed enterprises, the metallurgy workshop Equipetrol and the manufacturer of refractory material, Calderys, who had helped Indorca workers in their hour of need. Then the team of workers from these three workshops set off in a microbus to the coast. What resulted was a five-day solidarity "battle" at La Gaviota, which after some ups and downs, including some skepticism from the on-site workers, got the sardine factory fully running again in 2016. This was, for all intents and purposes, the first step toward forming the still to be named Productive Workers Army. The Battle of La Gaviota was the fledgling battle of this non-conventional army.

Learning, Planning, and Working Together

The guiding values that had emerged in the practice of self-management at the Indorca atelier—including equality, horizontality, democracy, and transparency—are all on display when, shortly after touring the business's heavy machinery hangar, we are able to attend Indorca's monthly all-staff meeting. This assembly, which takes place over an entire morning, with the whole staff arrayed around a conference table facing a giant whiteboard, is impressive if low-key. There, both workers and administrators see each other face to face, discuss, debate, and plan. In the meeting, one can see how *transparency* expresses itself in this organization, with every expense and every entry in the budget, past and future, painstakingly explained to all workers on the whiteboard. Similarly, the organization's commitment to *equality* means that all employees receive the same pay, while *democratic horizontality* is interpreted as ensuring that the main decisions are taken by vote after long debates conducted in the assembly.

Beyond these core values at Indorca, there is also a profound spirit of camaraderie and self-sacrifice, both in the rank and file and in the political cadres that work here.

One of the most important of these cadres, who has made substantial sacrifices for both Indorca and its project of the Productive Workers Army, is Sergio Requena. After the monthly staff meeting concludes around midday, we are able to interview him about his role in the project. A native of the Guayana zone, Requena received a university education and went on to occupy important roles in the state bureaucracy, the highest of which saw him heading the institution CORPIVENSA, charged with overseeing some two hundred new enterprises that the Bolivarian government wanted to foster. As often happens, a change in ministers saw Requena out of work, but rather than cool his heels in what would likely have been a comfortable middle-class existence, he offered his services as an educator to the workers struggling at Indorca. There he taught workers not only basic math skills, reading, and writing, but also revolutionary theory. Requena's selfless work as an educator and his inexhaustible enthusiasm quickly won over the hearts and minds of Indorca's workers. Shortly after, when the Productive Workers Army got going, he wholeheartedly joined the project and applied his energy and skills as a promoter and publicist for that new undertaking, including his set of influential contacts.

Requena has an evident passion for the Productive Workers Army. He picks up the story of this project, telling us how its solidarity brigades evolved in the wake of the battle at La Gaviota, its inaugural effort. That experience, especially the spirit of emulation it inspired in the workers in Cumaná, left the incipient Productive Workers Army eager to continue applying their skills to jump-starting industries with new "battles" in other locations. The next battles of the Productive Workers Army, relying on Requena's contacts, took a team composed of Indorca, Calderys, and Equipetrol workers all the way across the country to Barinas State, to a plant for making construction machinery and another that makes farm equipment. Here the workers had the honor of working in a project developed in Chávez's birthplace. The following year, 2017, saw a flurry of Productive Workers Army activity, including work on natural gas plants. By then the brigade had formally taken the name that it now bears. Requena tells us that they decided to call themselves a *productive* army to mark their difference from a military corps and yet highlight the fact that they were fighting a non-conventional war initiated by the United States with its sanctions and other aggressions against the people of Venezuela. For this reason, Requena refers to the project as "a non-conventional army in a non-conventional war."

A high point for many participants in the Productive Workers Army was working on the Amuay oil refinery, which is the third-largest refinery in the world and the largest in the Western Hemisphere. The sanctions had hit hard at this plant and left it functioning at reduced capacity, with its hydrogen compressors—equipment needed to desulfurize oil for making diesel and gasoline—completely stopped. They also needed help with repairing soldering equipment and their damaged ambulance. As before at La Gaviota, this time there was also skepticism from on-site workers. The employees at Amuay and especially the refinery's engineers felt that their expertise was being threatened by a bunch of unknown workers who, whatever practical know-how they had, did not have any formal degrees to show. Resistance was not only about dignity and expertise. There was also the tendency, widespread in state-run industries, to replace rather than repair broken equipment because of the kickbacks that new purchases permit. In effect, the management at Amuay did not want repairs because of their venality. Nevertheless, with patience and a certain amount of craftiness, the Productive Workers Army managed to overcome these internal obstacles. Requena tells us that he was particularly delighted to see how, when the bosses denied the brigade use of a forklift, a worker of Goliath-like proportions broke ranks with management and stepped in to lift the machinery himself. To Requena, this showed that even if management resisted, the workers at the refinery were committed patriots and revolutionaries!

NEW RULES, NEW PRACTICES

We have said that the Productive Workers Army contrives to change the rules of the game in an effort to break with the condition of dependency. What are those rules? Economic dependency is partly a result of the separation of workers, enterprises, and even countries that imperialism imposes, according to the time-tested method of *divide et impera*. That is, the weakness of dependent economies responds in great measure to a logic of atomization that capitalism generates both inside countries and among them. On a micro level, for example, it is easy to see how in a given neighborhood we often don't know what our neighbor does, what their skills are, and what they need. Instead, we turn to the market to get what we require and to solve our problems, and we expect our neighbor to do the same. In this way, we become more and more dependent on the market. On a larger scale, such atomization applies to whole countries that exchange with one another only insofar as it serves a particular niche determined by the world system's profit-making requirements. In peripheral countries, the logic of atomization reaches extremes, with each business existing as an oasis or enclave that is more connected to the global market than to what its neighbors do. Tellingly, it was when neighbors "broke the rules" of the market and pitched in to get Indorca going—particularly workers from Equipetrol and Calderys—that the idea for the solidarity brigades was born in this workshop's staff. They thought: *We have been helped by our neighbors in a spirit of solidarity that defies market relations, now where can we apply our own skills in a like manner?*

Requena, likely because of his work as a popular educator, uses plain language to describe their new practices of solidarity. He calls the process of reaching out to one's neighbor, whether an enterprise or individual, "crossing the street (*cruzando la calle*)." This kind of reaching out becomes especially important as a means of overcoming the situation in which there are two businesses that engage in complementary activities, literally often on opposite sides of the street in Guayana's industrial zone, yet each works in a kind of bubble. Crossing the street, then, is what got Indorca going again when its owner tried lockout and sabotage to stop the process of worker control. Workers from nearby Equipetrol and Calderys came over to lend them a hand. Then, Indorca workers returned the favor by crossing a street that is as wide as the country to get some fifteen other enterprises going with the Productive Workers Army. "Capitalism fragments everything and each business has its own little ruler," Requena says. "The main problem is that there isn't a centralized production plan, but add to that the fact that within the crisis, and the disorder that comes with it, some particular economic interests have surfaced, and you get the picture."

Requena is conscious that breaking down these barriers, overcoming what he calls "the archipelago logic," is far from easy, and often nothing short of a heroic task. For this reason, he compares the Productive Workers Army to the "epic feat" of Simón Bolívar sending a liberating army around Latin America two centuries ago, to free other countries after Venezuelan emancipation had been achieved. However, the parallels reach even deeper in Requena's view, for just as for Bolívar and his emancipating army, morale was a key factor, so the workers in the Productive Workers Army conceive their project as not just repairing machinery, but also *repairing consciousness.* They try to teach by example and in so doing raise people's morale, instilling the socialist and communal principles that their own volunteer work embodies.

These principles, including mutual encouragement and two-way learning, came to a head in the thirteenth battle that the Productive Workers Army undertook. This battle was also the first to be staged in an up-and-running commune. It occurred at El Maizal (chapter 1), which is probably the most consolidated rural commune in the country, with a solid project and a committed set of communards to back it up. As such, El Maizal is far from the creeping desperation that now affects many Venezuelans in either urban or rural contexts. Nevertheless, the presence of volunteer workers who helped them repair their mechanical milkers and refrigeration units, along with a tractor and an electrical manger, in early 2019, served as a wake-up call, broadening their horizons, and spurring their ambitions. This project brought revolutionary industrial and agricultural workers together for the first time, and the results were promising.

Winds of Change

There is a long history of organizing volunteer work in the revolutionary left, reaching from Lenin's Red Saturdays to the Chinese brigades of the Great Leap Forward to the Cuban Revolution. It is well known, partly because of an excellent photographic record, that Che Guevara during his time in Cuba put great emphasis on voluntary labor as a means of generating a new attitude toward work and transforming the human subjects themselves. Guevara not only participated in voluntary work himself, driving tractors and cutting cane, never shirking the most difficult tasks, but he also theorized its importance, emphasizing voluntary work's role in forming socialist consciousness. He called voluntary labor "a school for creating consciousness."[4] Che's idea responds to a longstanding concern in the Marxist tradition: how to transform people in a society in which all of us are organized by the logic of capital. Che, following theses developed by Marx, believed that such transformation is done through revolutionary praxis, especially cooperative work of the kind that the Productive Workers Army has carried out and attempted to inspire in its trips around the country. In these five- to seven-day stints, selfless collective work activities help generate the new human beings who work for social rather than selfish reasons, even as the values expressed in these work contexts foreshadow a future society based on superior social relations. By breaking the rules of the capitalist game in even a small corner of the world—as the Productive Workers Army has done—one opens a window in consciousness on the new society we can build.

No society is static, least of all one that has undergone a recent revolutionary transformation. Today there are winds of change blowing in Venezuela and an economic recovery is said to be taking place throughout the country. This recovery is visible and real, even if its bases are somewhat mysterious and it is experienced unequally, with some, mostly middle-class Venezuelans obtaining the resources to buy new vehicles and open new businesses, while others lag behind and find themselves in a country that offers limited education and precarious health services, while facing a host of bureaucratic issues that have been exacerbated by the blockade. In Indorca, we can see how the winds of recovery are bringing the possibility of new and more contracts, better salaries, and plans for expansion. This can be seen on the shop floor, where things are evidently picking up, and also in the offices where new plans are being laid. A brighter, if clearly still precarious future is showing its head, which will translate into expanded production, involve more workers, and recover employees' benefits.

In these future scenarios, the Productive Workers Army, which to date has carried out fifteen battles in different state-owned or worker-run enterprises and communes, could also play an important role, with its brigades being activated and even amplified in future scenarios. The economic recovery that is part of the new national context should be viewed with a critical eye. Its uneven nature and essentially capitalist character have become increasingly evident to Cira and me, in part because of the hard situation of many rural producers in the communes we've visited in our travels. For this reason, in our last conversations with Cedeño and Requena in the Indorca offices, we discuss the problems of the Cinco Fortalezas Commune in Cumanacoa, which we visited just a month before, and its inability to process the sugarcane that lies unharvested in its fields because of a broken sugar mill. They are interested by the project. With this in mind, a plan is beginning to take shape to organize the Productive Workers Army's sixteenth battle in this needy but combative commune.

There is also the possibility, which we discuss with them, of working with the newly founded Communard Union to coordinate the Workers Army's solidarity brigades. The linkages that the Union is now generating among communes could give the Productive Workers Army a clearer picture of where its efforts can be most useful. Here there seems to be enormous potential and the Workers Army's battles could eventually involve thousands of workers working hand-in-hand with communards. In this way, the web of communes that Chávez saw as a necessary step in the socialist transformation could benefit from the skill and above all the revolutionary spirit of these committed industrial workers, who rather than attempting to merely overcome the country's dependency in relation to the centers of capitalism, are now working to change the rules of the game entirely through the new labor relations this project embodies. These relations—admittedly in a small, if potentially expandable microcosm—constitute an emergent sociality in which the polarizing terms of dependence, centrality, and subordination are being replaced by a new way of relating on the basis of solidarity, mutuality, and complementarity.

8

El Panal Commune: Seething with Popular Power

The barrios of Venezuela's largest cities have long fascinated visitors from around the world. Caracas, the capital, has working-class barrios consisting of huge tracts of improvised construction that cover the hillsides in a seemingly endless labyrinth of houses and stairways. The houses are built from simple materials—cement or clay blocks are the most common, along with scavenged tie-bar and steel beams—but as self-built structures, they show what appears to be unlimited creativity and innovation. The result is a harlequin landscape made up of Escher-like constructions that twist and creep around the irregular terrain and are sometimes even cantilevered over the slopes. The irregularity of the buildings and the immense scale of the patchwork conglomerate they compose make an impression of sublimity on almost all who see these hillside barrios. Surveying a barrio from the windows of a highrise hotel or modern highway, visitors from other countries and social classes encounter an urban landscape that surprises them, offering a slightly overwhelming but also pleasant frisson. What

European Romantics experienced some two hundred years ago before snowy mountain peaks or huge cascades of water, that quickening of the heart and emptiness in the gut, is relived when overlooking these humanly made, awe-inspiring panoramas.

These barrios grew up with the depopulation of Venezuela's rural areas during the second half of the twentieth century. Rural to urban migration was a process that affected all Latin American countries in different degrees and with varied timeframes. However, in Venezuela, the migration process was particularly rapid due to the impact of the oil industry. Oil profits in a country that for forty years was the world's main oil exporter, and continues to have the world's largest proven reserves, made all other economic activities pale by comparison to what the "black gold" could generate. This imbalance in the economy is sometimes called the "Dutch disease" (in reference to how natural gas exploitation impacted the Netherlands), but the problem is structural, and more endemic to Venezuela than any other country. The widespread practice of importing food with petrodollars strangled much of the country's agriculture during the twentieth century, which survived mostly in a few specialized sectors along with low-intensity subsistence plots called *conucos*. From the rural wastelands, large masses of people began to flow to the cities, looking for education, health services, and work. Their expectations often met with disappointment. Sometimes—and these were the best jobs—they found employment in construction, but more often they had to turn to micro-commerce, odd jobs, or petty crime. If lucky, a young family member might obtain low-level employment in public administration, which could provide a constant, if limited, income to be shared in the family.

Most of the poor barrios of Caracas were built by a process popularly known as "*invasión*." People coming from the rural areas would occupy a tract of unused land, usually on a hillside. They would enter by night and prepare themselves to resist the combined repression from the "forces of order" and private owners in the upcoming days. They first built improvised and fragile houses, with "*techos de cartón*" (cardboard roofs), in the phrase made famous by Venezuela's revolutionary songwriter Alí Primera. With time, they reinforced these initial structures with brick and steel. The new residents would later divert electricity from the municipal system and begin to develop crude plumbing. Like all migrants, these people came not as mere biological beings but as multidimensional bearers of their cultures and life practices. What is remarkable, however, among Venezuela's rural-to-urban migrants is how so many aspects of their traditional rural lifestyle, formed over the *longue durée*, proved to be more resilient than those of their sisters and brothers in nineteenth-century European cities. For example, rural habits, such as early waking and early bedtimes, persisted in these barrios, and the same could be said for rural values such as solidarity, reciprocity, and a suspicion of those who enriched themselves.

VILLE RADIEUSE

The history of Venezuelan politics is spotted with governmental efforts to eliminate the poor hillside barrios, or what the newspapers came to call "rings of urban misery." The 23 de Enero barrio in the west of Caracas, famous today for its revolutionary activity, is the surprising result of one of these reform efforts. Beginning in the 1950s, it became the site of a massive construction project, consisting of some thirty large residential blocks that together could house almost 100,000 people. The project was initially conceived by dictator Marcos Pérez Jiménez, with the aim of providing residences for soldiers and people close to the government, while displacing poor people out of the zone. The idea of the nerdy dictator (Pérez Jiménez was legendary for his high grades in the military academy) was to build a *ville radieuse* on the Le Corbusier model—a radiant city with open sightlines and clear spaces between tall residential blocks. He imagined obedient soldiers and their families living quietly under the despotically imposed "order and progress" of a regime that so far had successfully contained class struggle. However, history had something else in store. The project conceived by the dictator would soon be occupied by desperate masses from around the area, who "invaded" the buildings and then had them renamed from "December 2" (the day the dictator's rule began) for the very day that a popular uprising took him down: January 23, 1958.

Nevertheless, things were not easy in the new epoch that began after the fall of the dictator, since the elected governments that came next were not much better. Under the restricted, even farcical, democracy of Venezuela's Fourth Republic (1958–1998), everything proved to be a struggle for the new inhabitants of the 23 de Enero housing blocks and the poor of Caracas more generally. They had occupied the modern buildings but had to clamor to obtain water, electricity, and basic services. The constant protests they carried out and the rural sociality they brought with them meant that these neighborhoods never became spaces of social isolation and estrangement. In this sense, they differed markedly from the panoptic urban spaces in the Global North that, in terms of infrastructure, they superficially resemble. Nor do they repeat the logic of the residential zones of the early industrial cities in Europe, such as the poor sections of Manchester where Frederick Engels felt that people "had been forced to sacrifice the best qualities of their human nature" and there was an "unfeeling isolation of each in his private interest."[1] Latin American urbanism in the twentieth century, even in modernized zones designed for social control, was markedly different from such European precedents, for here every space of the neighborhood was overflowing with irrepressible social life.

The life of the barrio included commerce, cultural and musical groups, community radios, but also, given 23 de Enero's history, revolutionary political organization. If this barrio had played a key role in taking down the dictator and in fighting to secure services for its residents after his fall, its work in favor of social justice did not stop there. The struggles of its residents expanded in the upcoming decades and took on organic form. The strength of these communities was such that the occupied buildings became the site of numerous popular power initiatives, while many of the barrio's grassroots organizations—usually referred to with the umbrella term *"colectivos"* (collectives) in the mainstream discourse—took on a more overtly political and sometimes explicitly communist character. Many of these collectives struggled against the closely paired combo of police repression and the drug trade. The first of the socially conscious local organizations to emerge that had a clear Marxist and internationalist calling was the Coordinadora Simón Bolívar, which was important in the struggles of the 1990s and in the early years of the Bolivarian Process. However, it was an excision from the Coordinadora, led by the creative and charismatic Robert Longa, that would prove to have greater staying power. Longa's organization, called Alexis Vive, would give rise to the El Panal Commune in 2006, which is far and above the most successful and fascinating of Venezuela's urban communes.

Parallel Lives

Robert Longa was a rebellious kid, even thrown out of the house and later put in jail for his rebelliousness. The whole social context at that time of fake, pro-imperialist democracy was so rife with injustices that it blurred the boundaries between crime, rebellion, and revolution. That was because, whether you followed the rules or not, you could count on the police coming for you. The system crushed people indifferently, not bothering to investigate first whether they were law abiding or not. It was an extreme situation that made rebellion a duty and defiance a point of honor. For example, when a group of barrio kids like Longa raided an ice-cream truck and shared its contents among friends and comrades, it was an action that crossed over between the categories of law breaking, self-empowerment, and reparations.

Probably no writer has grasped this as fully as Victor Hugo. For the great author of *Les Misérables*, injustice was above all something felt, and sentiment was at the center of his vision of human society, both the bad and the good in it. So, too, for Robert Longa, who says today that the revolutionary organization he founded and named in honor of his dead mentor Alexis González, is above all "a sentiment." That sentiment extends to the organization's clothing. Born among concrete towers that block out the sunlight, Alexis Vive militants always wear baby blue shirts that Longa told me stand for "open skies, dreams, and hope."

Tossed out onto the street when he was just fourteen years old, Longa lived in a machine room above an elevator shaft in one of the huge apartment blocks of 23 de Enero. He conspired in this tiny space with his friends, reading as much as he could lay his hands on. Longa always had Che Guevara nearby, both on the wall in a photo and close to his heart as an ideal. He loved Che. Then when Hugo Chávez came onto the scene, he fell for him too. Now in his mid-forties, Longa says he would rather die than betray the now-deceased revolutionary leader. In fact, Longa's and Chávez's lives were lived out with a strange synchronicity, strange parallels. Longa was sent to Yare Prison near Caracas, where Chávez had ended up after his 1992 uprising. Then, in 1999, Longa's release from Yare coincided with Chávez's election to the presidency. These kindred spirits were not only in tune but both were on the rise. Each began a process of building. For Longa, this meant building an organization in the barrio where he was born, first making the revolutionary *colectivo* Alexis Vive in 2001, then five years later El Panal Commune. As its first project, the Alexis Vive collective initially took on running drug traffickers out of the zone, eliminating a scourge that the powers that be and police had collaborated to introduce in the barrio in the 1980s and '90s to quell its revolutionary spirit. Alexis Vive needed to wipe the slate clean, but that was just the first step in a long, ongoing process of community construction.

THE COMMUNE'S HEADQUARTERS

The headquarters of the Alexis Vive collective is a narrow three-story building huddled next to a roofed basketball court, all of it in the shadow of a large tower block. You get to it by taking a turn off the main road that leads into 23 de Enero from the subway station, then passing under an archway that reads *"Bienvenidos, Comuna Socialista El Panal 2021."* The path takes you by a strip mall, then between narrow apartment blocks and an empty lot with a hexagonal Cuban Barrio Adentro module squatting in one corner. A strange silence and uncommon orderliness reigns in the zone, very different from most Caracas barrios. There is a reason for this: a keen observer might register that, along with a scattering of honeycomb graffities that have been painted along the way, discreetly placed CCTV cameras are at key points on the path. This is how the forty or so cadres of Alexis Vive monitor the zone from their headquarters and ensure that drug-trafficking organizations, and most likely even the police, do not enter the hard-won territory they have controlled for some twenty years.

The Alexis Vive headquarters is an office space located on the second floor of this building, which also houses the organization's "Arsenal" radio station and, just underneath, its deep-litter pig pen. The office comprises the 300 square feet where Robert Longa now leads most of his life. Security issues have dictated this lifestyle for him, since chasing out powerful narcos and their police allies from the barrio has left behind a trail of potentially lethal vendettas. The most notable things in the office, apart from Longa's imposing presence, are a lapdog named Plekhanov and a large portrait of Che, which is on a wall opposite the monitor that draws the feeds from the CCTV cameras. With a beefy six-foot frame, Longa is big for a Venezuelan who grew up in the poor barrios. His friends call him El Ruso (the Russian) when they do not call him "El comandante." If you ask Longa what inspired his group to get a head start in building a commune—beginning to do so even before Chávez made the communes an official state project around 2009—he will say that they built their flagship commune as simply an extension of "the model that Chávez defined as participative and protagonistic democracy." Apart from that, they were inspired by the Paris Commune, adapting its model of self-government to their "own space, time, and reality." At least, this is how Longa sees things, who views his historic role as that of putting Marxism-Leninism at the service of popular power.

The first concrete and visible step toward building the El Panal Commune occurred in 2006 when a private construction firm was working in the barrio. The Alexis Vive collective leaned on them to build the arch for the commune at the entrance, the one with the inscription saying "Welcome to El Panal Commune 2021." In effect, they made the construction firm carry out a social project based on the 2 percent of their budget that Venezuelan law mandates all state-contracted firms should direct to community projects. This gesture—of applying at least the threat of force to make sure the law was carried out—was in some ways a repetition of what Alexis Vive had done to get corrupt police and drug traffickers out of the neighborhood because they had set the barrio back so much in terms of popular power and revolutionary organization in the 1980s and '90s. Then too, they had worked mostly with persuasion, as when they had projected movies in public spaces formerly used for the narcotics trade, while helping the dealers find other jobs. However, as everyone knew, the Alexis Vive collective had the organizational strength and even the firepower to back up its proposals.[2]

Yet the communal arch was only an outward sign of a deeper organizational process underway. That process eventually brought together the eight communal councils in the zone into the new El Panal Commune, guaranteeing its economic viability by linking the incipient commune to a socially owned bakery that offered large volumes of rigorously price-controlled bread to folks in the neighborhood, along with a now defunct sugar-packing business that is soon to become an animal feed plant. Longa may have masterminded this project, but he believes that the community should take the initiative of involving itself in the commune, with the organizational vanguard, Alexis Vive, working mostly to encourage people to commit themselves, convincing them to take charge of their lives and their community.

The robust commune that exists today speaks for the correctness of Longa's wager: El Panal is the most consolidated and ambitious urban commune in Venezuela, even if the beginnings of the project were humble, with much of the work of winning over hearts and minds for the project being done with volunteer activities that he and his closest comrades did, like cleaning stairways of the apartment blocks, which were always sore points in the community. Throughout, the process of constructing the commune has been maintained by Longa's total faith in Chávez's strategy of socialist construction. Asked if it is possible to build socialism through the commune, Longa brightens up and smiles: "Not only is it *possible*, but we are convinced that it is the correct line. It is the most efficient and effective way to build the model the Chávez defined."

ANACAONA

The commune they have built is called *El Panal* (The Beehive) because bees do hard, collective work. Indeed, a deeply ingrained work ethic is evident in this commune where the militants—likely as a deliberate affront to mainstream values—usually sport stained clothing and dirty shoes, and they never stop moving about and multitasking. This is the case with Bárbara "Anacaona" Martínez, who is Longa's second-in-command in the Alexis Vive collective and a main organizer of the El Panal Commune. In her tattered baby blue shirt and worn-out sneakers, Martínez is rarely inactive for even a moment: she seems to be constantly greeting people from the barrio who pass by, while never ceasing to send text messages right and left about pressing business. Cira and I have just managed to corral this high-level Alexis Vive cadre for an interview in the bleachers of the basketball court. Yet as we begin chatting, a pair of bank employees from the city center show up on the other side of the court, to inspect the commune for a possible loan. They appear somewhat lost. Martínez shouts curt orders to them, telling the disoriented bankers where they can wait and find chairs. I can't help thinking that it is gratifying to be in a place where, contrary to the norm, it is the bankers who are made to wait for people!

Despite the interruption, Martínez has not lost the thread of her narrative, which weaves together complex ideas about socialist theory, the 23 de Enero barrio's history, and principles of communal organization into a seamless whole. Martínez's past is relevant, because she is not strictly speaking from the grassroots. She met Longa in the Sociology Department of the Universidad Central de Venezuela where they were both studying, and because of her talent and commitment, she was soon brought into the organization's leadership. As part of our investigation, we are interested in what this cadre can tell us about the relation between the vanguard organization, Alexis Vive, and the more inclusive project of building the El Panal Commune, as an expression of popular power. To explain why this vanguard has succeeded where others have failed, Martinez emphasizes that, as militants of Alexis Vive, they "are not extraterrestrials" but part of the community itself—she herself now lives in the Camboya neighborhood that is inside the commune. Their only distinction is that they belong to "a social and political organization that understands its role in the community." Moreover, Alexis Vive's aim is not to "appropriate people's participation" but rather to blend with the people. Much of this, she tells us, has to do with managing contradictions inside the community and simply accompanying them in processes of self-organization.

The Alexis Vive collective is a more or less vertical organization of cadres, not unlike a Leninist party. It has a strict sequence of command, with Martínez on the first tier, in what is called the *comandancia*. Though the command structure is directional, it is founded more on conscious discipline and moral example than blind obedience. Commands are conveyed through walkie-talkies that connect the main militants. The military nature of the organization and the power that afforded them allowed the collective to successfully free the barrio from drug mafias and police oppression and jump-start communal construction by a few years, well before Chávez started the nationwide drive. All of this was done in urban conditions that have proved to be over-whelming obstacles for other leftist groups in the country. Yet organizers like Martínez are completely aware that they cannot subordinate either the commune or community councils in the zone to their more tight-knit organization, Alexis Vive. To do so would be to nip popular power in the bud. This is where hard work, leading by example, and showing restraint comes in. The cadres of the organization do a great deal of manual work them-selves, taking on the hardest, dirtiest jobs. They want to be the first to arrive to any chore and the last to leave. Also, while there is always much to be done, nothing should be approached as a mere task. Rather, the trick, Martínez tells us, is to find the revo-lutionary side and strategic implications of every activity that appears along the way.

Leadership Examples

This organizational approach turns as much on prudent leader-ship as it is an interpretive task. Two incidents that I witnessed speak for the Alexis Vive collective's careful and creative modus operandi with the community. One involved a young Alexis Vive cadre, who was giving a tour to a group of community represen-tatives through the commune's different productive units. The tour was carefully done, and the dozen or so representatives were led from the bakery and textile factory to the fish farm and pigsty, with the young cadre explaining at each stop how things work in a technical sense. There were photos and laughter, and every-body was enjoying themselves a great deal. To me, it seemed to be a wonderful tour and all very well executed. Hence, I was surprised to find that Martínez had taken aside the young cadre and was criticizing him for making it into a mere museum tour. She insisted that there should be a process of formation and theoretical learning associated with each such experience, especially a visit from interested community members. The strategic aim of the commune and the relation of its productive projects to the socialist goal had been ignored. The young cadre had fallen into economism. As a corrective, Martínez suggested that everybody in the group learn something about productive forces and their connection to relations of production, and she pointed them to the relevant sections of Marta Harnecker's work, *The Basic Concepts of Historical Materialism.*

The second incident happened during the elections of communal council spokespeople. The elections occurred over the weekend, and conducting them was a massive operation involving some 10,000 potential voters, reaching to all the bases of the El Panal Commune and beyond. The Alexis Vive collective took charge of setting up polling stations and maintaining security, and even launched its own candidates for many positions. They did all the organizational work masterfully. The atmosphere during the voting process was good natured and festive, with enthusiastic participation and free soup doled out while people hung out near the polls, talking about barrio life and current events. Turnout was good too, reaching more than 40 percent of potential voters. However, at the end of the day, Alexis Vive's candidates did not always come out winners, and Robert Longa himself did not land the post he wanted in his communal council. Yet I was able to witness how Martínez took charge of the situation and spoke with a great deal of maturity and farsightedness about what the results meant for the commune's future. Her carefully chosen words were only constructive and advisory. In the spirit of counsel, she told the newly elected spokespeople that "they were not owners, not representatives, not a network, but spokespeople for the community." They were also advised that being a spokesperson was hard work and reminded that they could be revoked if they failed to carry out the mandate the community had given them.

Working alongside the community rather than outside it, Martínez clearly excels at sorting out contradictions among the people and giving a revolutionary reading to situations as they emerge in the barrio's organizational processes. Through her practice, one can see how important *interpretation* is to community leadership and revolutionary direction. Arguably, constructing a narrative so that people understand the strategic aim is the better part of community organization in many circumstances. For this reason, there is a constant effort at El Panal Commune to apply a political spin to any and every activity and thus drive home the strategic questions of "What is the commune?" and "What is the commune for?" In Martínez's words, which she makes good on through her coherent leadership style, Alexis Vive does not want to be a "vanguard that defines people's lives" but rather works so that "people are convinced and take charge of their own lives." They aim to meld with the people at the same time that they promote a logic where economics is consistently subordinated to politics—or one where "politics is in command"—to use the old Maoist maxim they have internalized.

When I think about the work being done here, it seems to me that it is the heroic narrative of epic dimensions, carefully constructed through an ongoing interpretive process, that keeps people going in this organization. It also forms the basis of their connection to the wider community. On a temporal axis, that narrative reaches back to the past, as Longa's comments indicate, and it expresses loyalty to Chávez while projecting his project forward into a socialist future. In a geographic sense, it weaves together the work of the smallest cell (in the beehive) to the region, the nation, and beyond. Cadres like Martínez work to develop and maintain this epic narrative, carefully subsuming each small step into its strategic architecture as a way of prefiguring the greater goal, which provides a social cement in the community and continuity for the project through time. Sadly, this kind of overarching epic narrative has generally been lacking in Venezuela since Chávez died, where both the government and people are operating most often in survival mode. Of course, El Panal Commune is also in this mode much of the time. However, survival here is always seen as a step toward something greater: toward emancipation, and not only in this small neck of the woods, but for Venezuela as a whole and internationally. The communards here try to make all the elements they develop on a micro or local scale fit into an overarching plan.

COMMUNAL PLANNING

Planning and communication are things that bees also do, though these features of the communal insect's behavior were unknown until scientists discovered their waggle dance in the mid-twentieth century. For example, Karl Marx was clearly limited by the science of his time when he contrasted honeybees with human architects, thinking that only the latter could plan something before doing it.[3] Of course, Marx was right about the praxis of the human being, which he wished to characterize as an animal capable of proposing and planning, even if he underestimated bees. In our time, however, the communards at El Panal, who have bees embroidered on their shirts and painted all over the walls of their barrio, are making good on the correct appreciation of the animal that gives their commune its name by engaging in detailed and ambitious planning of their projects. This applies most fully to the economic side of El Panal's work, whose largest planning framework, called the *Distrito Económico* (Economic District), goes hand in hand with sweeping notions of how to reindustrialize a wide zone that reaches outside the strict territory of the commune and into much of the west of Caracas.

El Panal's Economic District coordinates three main productive projects (fish farming, pig raising, textile production)—all of them expressions of socialist property and worker control—along with a handful of juridically private businesses that provide resources for the commune. At the center of the Economic District is a communal bank that has a role in organizing, planning, and developing projects in the zone. Having a communal bank to help with planning and coordination is a basic feature that El Panel Commune shares with most other communes in Venezuela, and it is part of the Law of Communes. The presence of a bank in these communes could seem odd. Yet it is not about market socialism, which is the very antithesis of the project of communal socialism with its strategic aim of completely overcoming the rule of value production. Quite the opposite: inasmuch as the communal banks coordinate resources for the productive projects that are under a commune's control, or are associated with it, they are transitory institutions that aim to keep market relations at bay as long as the communes, still making their first steps, are like socialist islands adrift in a capitalist sea where monetary relations will unfortunately persist during the course of the transition.

In El Panal, the communal bank, which at one time issued its own currency, is now focused on managing the range of projects that are included in the Distrito Económico: both the small businesses that are allied with the commune and provide it with resources and the strictly communal enterprises (EPSs) that operate under the framework of socialist property. According to Alexis Vive cadre Asdrúbal Rendon, nicknamed "Tijuana," the unique character of this grassroots institution has to do with its coordinating and allotting role. "The Communal Bank at El Panal does not suck the life out of the working class, like a traditional financial institution," he told me. "Instead, our bank is an arm of the Economic District, which is the organ that plans the commune's economy." This is aptly put, and it locates well the task that El Panal's communal bank aims to accomplish, inasmuch as it exists as a defensive and provisional firewall to the market relations that exist outside. During the transition to socialism, when finances and markets still permeate the remainder of society, such internal coordination of its funds may keep El Panal Commune from falling prey to financial systems that are all too willing to either crush or deform community projects and communal enterprises.[4]

ABEJITAS TEXTILE WORKSHOP

On our second day at the commune, we visit one of the communal enterprises that forms part of the Distrito Económico: a tailoring shop called Las Abejitas (little bees) of El Panal. The project is tucked into a former shopping mall a short walk from the building housing Longa's office. There, in a brightly lit space, are rows of industrial sewing machines alongside a colorful boutique with mannequins that display both the Abejitas line of work clothes and school uniforms and an array of casual everyday clothes. All the products sport El Panal commune's stylized bee logo: this icon consists of a striped teardrop that represents a bee's abdomen and stinger. On crossing the shop's threshold, flanked by images of Bolívar and Chávez, we are greeted by one of the workers, the fifty-something José Lugo. A former naval officer, Lugo was won over for the revolution when he saw the work of Cuban doctors in his own barrio, and he was in turn brought into the El Panel project when Robert Longa got in touch with him, around 2012. Now Lugo is working in this socialist enterprise with great enthusiasm. As someone who has traded arms for a sewing machine, he enjoys joking that imperialism was right about Venezuela when it declared the country to be an "extraordinary and unusual threat." Lugo generally points to the bays of sewing machines when saying so. "We are a terrible threat," he says with a chuckle, "not for any military reason, but because of the socialist example that is taking shape in projects like the one you are visiting!"

Accompanying Lugo in the shop today is Margarita Márquez, a longtime staff member here. She worked from her house as a tailor from the time she was just fifteen, joining the Abejitas textile project when her children were already adults. Tailoring is wide-spread in the barrios, so it was a natural transition for Márquez, Lugo, and others to organize the work as a communal business, a social property enterprise. The market for these textile products, the profits from which are managed by the communal bank, are both individuals and private and public institutions, such as the contract they once had to make uniforms for a small airport near Caracas and another more recent commission for shirts from the Ministry of Communes. Márquez takes a pause from her work to tell us how she likes the shop-floor environment here, which has helped her develop as a person. A key benefit is that the workers at Abejitas do varied tasks and thereby learn about the entire production process, which helps break down the fragmentation of knowledge and skills that comes with the capitalist division of labor. "I don't like the idea of working for a private business," Márquez says, "since it means spending the whole day seated at one place and doing one task. I feel very comfortable here. It's like my second home."

Along with personal development based on learning new skills—remember that Marx in the *Grundrisse* said that "real wealth is the developed productive power of all individuals"[5]—Márquez points to how this communal enterprise has given workers like her recognition from the community and even resulted in her appearing on public television. This is one worker's lived experience of communal socialism—socialism seen from the inside!—and it has as much to do with affect and dignity as it does with the end of economic exploitation. It is interesting that when you ask Márquez, Lugo, or other workers about what makes this small enterprise *socialist*, all will put emphasis on details such as the pleasant work environment and the free snacks that we are now munching on with the workers. They will point to how in the Abejitas workshop there are no restrictions on how many times you can go to the bathroom or how often you can use your telephone, and the overall environment is friendly. In their vision of socialist work, qualitative aspects, as opposed to quantitative ones, come to the foreground. The Abejitas workers' internally developed value system, which puts emphasis on a pleasing environment and humanly gratifying activity, is typical of the language used in the Chavista grassroots to refer to socialism and describe the world they want. For example, one hears from most workers that such and such an activity or project isn't *capitalist* but *socialist,* while what they identify as socialist features is not so much equal salaries, which do, in fact, exist here, but rather how the project helps the community, treats people fairly and gently, and provides human comforts.

Dogmatists might consider this quaint, because, armed with what they believe to be "socialist science," they reduce socialism to simply the end of exploitation and relegate the rest to mere decoration and "feel-good" details. Socialism, in this view, has a hard core, which in their interpretation of social ownership, is delivering simply more value, or even the whole of the value produced, to the workers. But they would be wrong, for a conception of socialism that is based only on a fair distribution of economic value is problematic, because it falls short of what is needed.[6] It would be far better to conceive socialist emancipation in terms that center non-alienated labor and internal democracy, along with forms of labor and social life more generally that are not subsumed under the logic of capitalist value relations. For it is precisely through de-alienated, directly social labor, along with substantial, democratic control of one's labor activities and products; and it is precisely by cultivating humanly enjoyable and meaningful forms of interaction on a capillary level both in workplaces and communities that the logic of capital (and economic exploitation, too) can be completely eradicated from society. So, Venezuela's grassroots militants, with their homegrown discourse based on experience more than books, actually have a great deal of socialist science on their side. They are correct to bring pleasure and de-alienation, along with internal democracy, to the forefront of their vision of socialism. This is the essence of Marx's scientific approach to socialism, and in other passages of the *Grundrisse* and *Capital,* he refers to wealth as including the "universality of the individual's needs, capacities, [and] *enjoyments*," while claiming that "capitalism is already abolished once we assume that it is *enjoyment* that is the driving principle and not enrichment itself."[7]

Year Zero

Sometimes the true dimensions of contemporary events can best be perceived with comparisons. Arguably, the sanctions the United States has imposed on Venezuela since 2015 can be compared to putting the entire population of the country—including children, the old, and the sick—in a concentration camp. Under the regime of sanctions, every day brought a new turn of the screw for the population, in a context defined by scarce food, daily deaths, and almost no light at the end of the tunnel. One looked around and saw the clothes falling off people, dazed patients without medication wandering the streets, families making desperate plans to migrate, and one got the distinct feeling that the depths of human cruelty were being probed. What were these ruthless coercive economic measures for? The experience could leave you feeling paralyzed. What possible motive could make a powerful country want to decimate the population of another? Was it for their sin of being born Venezuelans, just as in the last century others were persecuted and murdered for being Jews or Armenians? Thinking about the U.S. blockade could leave you feeling nonplussed, empty, and hopeless. The Alexis Vive collective understood the danger of this psychological state. Its leader Robert Longa told me that, after a prolonged stay in a rural zone during the early years of the blockade, he returned to the barrio and found that people had a distant, glazed look in their eyes. Somehow there had to be a way to get people snapped out of their hypnosis and begin to struggle, even if symbolically. That was when Longa came up with the idea of declaring 2020 to be "Year Zero" for the commune; it meant that what looked like the end could also be seen as a beginning.

That was the year the commune decided to expand. More than a traditional revolutionary leader, Longa felt he was a kind of poet-in-residence, whose job was raising people's morale and animating those whose spirits had fallen. For example, he conceived the idea in reference to the pandemic that instead of "staying at home" (as the authorities had directed) people should "stay in the commune." He also riffed on Bolívar's quote about struggling against disobedient nature if it opposes us, saying instead that if *disease and hunger* oppose us, we will struggle against them. Beyond these symbolic gestures, there was real work and expansion of the commune's projects on various levels. Since the zone's community councils, the basis of communal construction, had been on hold by governmental decree since 2014, Longa's cadres invented the surrogate organizational format of "Panalitos," and used it to expand popular power in the nearby barrios. Because schooling was closed, they developed the "Pluriversidad" as a self-organized higher education project. The communards also strove to expand their work on productive fronts, with new pig and fish farming projects in the barrio, and they sent brigades to some rural plots they had acquired in Miranda and Lara states and began—in the face of numerous difficulties (especially their lack of knowledge of agriculture)—to work there too. The truth is that from "zero," there is nowhere else to go. The only thing you can do is keep on adding!

TOWARD A BRIGHTER FUTURE

Jorge Quereguan is a main cadre of Alexis Vive. He came from one of the organization's satellite cells in the western city of Valencia to militate in Caracas's El Panal Commune during the blockade and pandemic years. On the morning of our third day visiting the commune, we encounter him in mud-stained clothes, after having spent a night mucking out the pig pens under Longa's office. Quereguan was exhausted but in good spirits, having worked from dusk till dawn to replace the coffee hulls that function as litter in the deep-bed pens. The state of his clothes has piqued our interest and makes us inquire into what was behind his having to pull an all-nighter. What seems to have happened is that some workers from the community had begun the chore of cleaning the pig pens, yet they signed off when the sun went down. However, true to the organization's ethic, Quereguan felt that he had to set a revolutionary example, and that meant staying till he had finished the job!

Between sips of his morning coffee, Quereguan goes into some detail explaining this commune's progress on productive fronts: the steps they have taken in economic terms from the fresh starting point that "Year Zero" (or 2020, which was the hardest year they lived through) represented for this committed group of communards. When Quereguan tells this story, I can perceive important similarities with the Great Leap Forward (1958–62), when the first Chinese communes were built. Just as in that massive drive for "accelerated socialist construction" in China some sixty years ago, the methodology that the Alexis Vive collective promoted in Caracas was for people to throw themselves into productive projects, experiment, learn by doing, and even learn from errors. Of course, the historical evaluation of the Great Leap is highly contested, as it should be, given the widespread starvation that occurred at the same time. However, it must be kept in mind that, despite the many errors and tragic loss of life, the Great Leap Forward represented a time when numerous people, especially in rural areas, broke out of the narrow routines that had characterized their lives and grew as individuals and revolutionaries. For many in China, it was their own "Year Zero" and, among other things, an important step in terms of personal development.[8]

Quereguan tells us how the urban pig farming project was born in this context of revolutionary experimentation. As part of a plan to feed the community, El Panal Commune had brought some pigs to Caracas to slaughter them. On discovering that one of the sows was pregnant, they let it give birth in Longa's kitchen, and began to raise the animals, experimenting with a variety of foods as alternatives to commercial feed. All their information came from trial and error or from watching videos and reading online. The same could be said for the fish farming project that also got going that year: they simply began by throwing some tilapia minnows into an abandoned, unused pool. There was more watching of videos online and many failures. Later the communards got some support from the government to build neat cylindrical tanks, made of wire and plastic sheeting, with freshwater feeds, which they now expect could yield up to 200 kilos of fresh fish every month.

Quereguan tells us how, in all of this experimentation, the "genius of the people" and the "will of the cadre" are key. Trial by error and empirical discoveries are followed by technification of the production processes. Now El Panal's pig pen, which is based on Cuban deep litter methods that were widely used in urban areas during the Special Period, has more than eighty pigs and they are developing plans for processing their own sausages and cold cuts. This way of working inevitably implies that the commune has a host of false starts and failures behind it. Yet it has constantly sought a way forward and has always relied on what it calls "the creative powers of the people," who learn and gain confidence through the experience. Overall, the commune's work since Year Zero has been a process of maturation for militants and community members, who have been put to the test along the way and have consistently risen to the occasion. In that spirit, Quereguan tells us: "We cannot fail, we cannot let a few failures call into question the goal of the commune. That is because it is *the hour of the commune*."

During the interview, an electric tricycle, towing a cart heaped with plastic and cardboard waste, pulls up. This is the commune's latest project: collecting plastic and electrical appliances and recycling them. Here again the social and political is combined with the economic. The recycling project will generate revenues, but it is also aimed at giving jobs to youths who are at loose ends and might feel they have few options other than crime. Quereguan explains that this is part of the commune's security plans, which are not based on repression, like those of the state, but involve finding alternatives that respond to the roots of crime and encourage community participation. Indeed, the threesome who are unloading the plastic bottles appear happy to be doing something useful. Driving the electric tricycle, which they seem to approach as a novel kind of motorbike, works as a giant plus too. All of it points to how a situation where the police don't show their faces is much better for everyone. Without the presence of policing forces in this barrio—from which neighbors formerly needed to defend themselves—this community has developed an efficient internal security system that is about the neighbors themselves taking charge of what occurs, and responding in thoughtful ways to incidents and problems as they arise.

This flagship urban commune has scored victories in a number of areas, such as production, self-managed security, and education. To everyone's evident relief, the most oppressive features of the state apparatus are now either held at bay or made to serve the people, and there is a light at the end of the tunnel as far as the most basic economic issues are concerned. All the while, popular power is emerging from the doors that have been opened for it by a vanguard organization that shows commitment to the people and political clarity. The relaxed atmosphere in the zone speaks for this. The barrio fairly seethes with expressions of local empowerment, which also reveals itself in people's confident, calm, and cooperative attitudes, as well as in the harmonious coexistence that exists on the streets. For example, from the bench where we are chatting with Quereguan, a COVID vaccine operation can be seen happening in a nearby plaza, while kids are repairing bikes and others are playing chess nearby. Overall, one senses that an entire weight has been lifted from this urban community—the weight of historical injustice, imperialist oppression, capitalist exploitation, and police repression—and with this weight lifted, the intrinsic, multiple, and varied powers of the people are emerging. It took the spark of a vanguard organization with seasoned militants, to clear the path and point to the alternative that communal construction provides. However, today in this neighborhood where both the tower blocks and state repression once cast such long shadows, the blue sky of "dreams and hope" symbolized in the baby-blue shirts of Alexis Vive militants seems to be opening up for a large and growing community.

9

Epilogue: Looking Back, Looking Forward

A white-haired, properly dressed man entering the eighth decade of life came back to Caracas from the east of Venezuela, where he had been farming for several years. A friend drove him to the capital city, whose high buildings between blue-green mountains he had not seen for some time. He stayed at his daughter's apartment in the middle-class section of town. The old man set up shop in the basement of a new experimental university housed in a former Shell Oil headquarters, the Universidad Bolivariana de Venezuela, where the rector had given him an office by the university's printshop. There he received people from all walks of life. This soft-spoken but confident man was especially interested in talking to the diverse members of the student body that the new university, founded in revolution, had brought together, but he also received other visitors, including famous MPs and high government officials in his den in the university's basement. This was around 2003 and the man was Carlos Betancourt.

Betancourt, also known as "Comandante Jerónimo," had been at war with just about everything since he was a kid. His first political act, as a high school student in the 1950s, was handwriting one-sheet flyers that said, "Down with the dictator!" which he did until a Communist Party member took him aside and told him there were better ways of achieving the same end. He began participating in revolutionary organizations struggling to overthrow Pérez Jiménez. Later, with the betrayal of the left-wing and center-left coalition that brought down the dictatorship and the consolidation of the false democracy, Betancourt became, like many others at that time, a *guerrillero*. At first, because of his good handwriting, he was taken on as the secretary of the FALN guerrilla's maximum leader Argimiro Gabaldón, but he eventually became commander of an eastern front in the area where he was born. His front held out very long because of his skill with logistics such as burying canned food supplies and helping the wounded. When most of the guerrilla disbanded in the 1970s, Betancourt shifted gears and formed a new clandestine organization, *Bandera Roja*, which was the scourge of the sold-out establishment and its collaborators for the last decades of the twentieth century. The organization turned to the right in the 1990s, but before that happened Betancourt jumped ship and began farming in Monagas State. Nonetheless, he kept in touch with developments in the country and was continuously thinking and reading.

When he came back to Caracas, Betancourt was an old man, but he had a new idea. He had seen how Chavismo was founding socialist enterprises, and yet perceived that the decision-making inside them was still largely vertical. Betancourt had always been an avid reader, and he was aware of writings by Marx where the concrete form of decision-making in labor contexts was taken to be more important than formal property relations. For this reason, and because he had always drawn from the legacy of Maoism, the old *guerrillero* began to promote horizontal decision-making and the commune as a model for production in the country. He called the new organization he was forming—the *raison d'être* of the interminable meetings he was holding in the basement of the university—the "Comuneros," and he published a periodical with the same name. Betancourt was indefatigable in pursuing the communard ideal. He met and talked with everybody, even building alliances with the hotheaded Marxist-Leninist "Gayones" group in Lara State and making visits to the Alexis Vive collective in 23 de Enero, where he may have been a key inspiration for that organization's early start in building El Panal Commune. In this way, Betancourt ceaselessly promoted direct democracy, popular power, the commune, and the idea of a "revolution inside the revolution"—all before these ideas had become important in Chávez's discourse and mainstream Chavismo.

The story of Betancourt—who died in 2021 of COVID complications, but never ceased promoting the communard project—is interesting because he was clearly a bellwether in tune with the needs of the people and country and because of his firsthand knowledge of Venezuela's past, having participated in fifty years of struggle for emancipation. Not only had Betancourt surveyed, through reading, the whole of the country's history, but he had lived a large part of it, too. He had tried everything, having been a student leader, a *guerrillero*, and a Maoist, and had also listened to everybody and tested most forms of struggle. Hence it is relevant and telling that, with Betancourt's extensive knowledge of the country and its history—and with his participation in many of the left's experiments, partial successes, and failures behind him—he finally opted for the commune, insisting on the importance of the communal path to socialism, with its project of self-emancipation through self-organization.

Gusts of History

I like to think of Betancourt as resembling the angel of history that Walter Benjamin wrote about in his *Theses on the Concept of History*. In this epoch-making document, the German-Jewish thinker refers to a Paul Klee painting that hung in his rooms. The painting is childlike and "primitive," showing a large-eyed, spread-eagle winged figure that is more Rorschach test-like than humanoid in some respects. Benjamin imagined Klee's angel, the *Angelus Novus*, along the lines of previous allegorical figures that represent history; such figures look back even as they move forward.[1] Looking back, the surprised angel surveys the panorama of history, but what he sees is an accumulation of ruin, not progress. In Benjamin's words, the angel confronts the "pile of debris" that is the past, and he sees "one single catastrophe which keeps piling wreckage and hurls it in front of his feet."[2] Nowhere is this imagined scenario of disaster more real than in Latin America, where every century and every decade seems to bring a new turn of the screw in an ongoing scenario of suffering, from the Monroe Doctrine and gunboat diplomacy to developmentalism, neoliberalism, and now sanctions. The string of disasters that is a constant in this continent's history is seemingly unending. Moreover, moving forward or "progressing" along the lines already established, as Benjamin correctly perceived, would only bring more disaster. Hence, a revolution means bringing things to a halt. For that reason, Benjamin equated the socialist revolution with *pulling the emergency brake*, in an appendix to the same brief document.

Benjamin may also be credited with being one of the most acute theorists of the profound relation between disaster and revolution. Disasters, whether natural or human-made or both, are terrible in that they bring death, injury, and trauma. However, they can also mark a new beginning. This is especially so when the disasters we experience are recognized as such. Here is where another of Benjamin's concepts comes in: *the real state of emergency*. Part of his idea in referring to the "real state of emergency" is that a crisis, which is what history has always been for the oppressed, could also become a point of emergence of the new.[3] The spark for this is often a literal and specific disaster, such as a war or natural catastrophe. In such conditions, the situation of the poor becomes explicit. Now, it is not only the Angel of History who sees the ruins that the past has hurled into the present, but the masses themselves. Indeed, most revolutions are born out of such disaster situations. The Russian and Chinese revolutions triumphed on the heels of devastating world wars, but it can also be an earthquake, which is what stands as a distant cause behind the 1978 Sandinista Revolution in Nicaragua. The critical issue, however, is always to reflect on the disaster, for only when the steps people take in the face of it—which usually express ingenuity, solidarity, and seeds of popular power—are thematized and reflected upon do they become lasting ones: part of a durable transformation and a roadmap for the future.

Disasters and Paradises

Reflecting on the disaster that has piled up in Venezuela's history and the need to put an end to it, as Carlos Betancourt did after a long life of struggle, has led numerous Venezuelans to opt, like him, for the commune. Indeed, in the various trips around Venezuela that are chronicled in this book, we have seen how ordinary Venezuelans responded to the latest episode of the country's historical disaster—the nationwide emergency represented by loss of leadership, cruel U.S. sanctions, and economic downturn—with solidarity and mutual aid, and with concrete steps in commune-building. This occurred, in diverse circumstances, whether urban or rural, whether in the center of the country or on its frontiers. For example, the country's profound crisis after Chávez's death is what provoked El Maizal Commune to expand by seizing idle land in its area. It impelled the Luisa Cáceres communards to occupy storefronts and begin garbage-collecting and recycling. And it led El Panal Commune to declare their situation to be "Year Zero." In the Guayana zone, the crisis encouraged industrial workers to respond to the solidarity they received from neighbors by developing their now legendary work brigades.

Something similar happens in many crises and disasters around the world, as Rebecca Solnit has documented in her wonderful book, A *Paradise Built in Hell*.[4] An earthquake, tsunami, or war

often promotes changes, opening a window on what we desire
and how we can achieve it. However, unlike other crisis situations
and disasters around the world, past and present, the Venezuelan
crisis of the 2010s had, in Chávez's legacy and his theorization
of the commune, an already existing roadmap. That roadmap
might have seemed somewhat irrelevant or at least too ethereal
when Chávez was alive and the petroleum boom persisted, but it
fit like a glove on the situation that emerged after his death. This
meant that Chávez's legacy was like a time capsule left behind
that was later unearthed in different parts of the country and put
to good use. The time capsule even included a set of more or
less forgotten but very advanced laws, the *Popular Power Laws* of
2010, which "authorized" such transformations. The ensemble
of this legacy meant that such steps as are taken in a spontaneous way in many crisis situations—growing food, intervening in
factories, and appropriating idle lands—could be understood
in post-Chávez Venezuela in terms of a strategic project. Each
small step could be ratcheted up toward a future that was already
mutually understood. Individual and dispersed actions fit into an
overarching project, and the different remedies people pursued
on a local level could be part of a meaningful revolution that was
radical insofar as it went to the roots of things.

CHANGING THE WHOLE GAME

A revolution is literally a *turning around*, but it is also a tre-
mendous shake-up. Mao Zedong said it was a great disorder,
followed by a new order. Lenin, following Marx, said that a
revolution was a change that goes beyond the actually existing
order of things. Almost everybody can see the need for such a
profound shake-up today. The innumerable problems we face,
whether social, economic, or environmental, all point to the need
for a profound change in our time, a time when billions of people
lack access to basic goods and services, and the environmental
crisis has reached a new level of urgency. However, the kind of

change needed is obviously one that must go beyond the *what* to the *how*, must reach beyond the *contents* to the *configuration*, and must change not only the *players* but the *rules* they play by. The point is that the main elements and actors in our reality are determined by unseen rules—their actions are channeled and not free—so it is these laws that must be changed if we want a different outcome.

Indeed, well-meaning social movements and political parties have tried to change discrete elements of our reality in the past, and yet the desired results were not brought about. So what is needed is a change in the rules of the game: a *game-changer*, in the most profound sense of that term. The key rule in that sense, the main determinant that must be changed, is the law of value, or the necessity of value production in the capital system. It is this invisible law that leads to the senseless production of non-necessary goods, the uncontrollable and dangerous expansiveness of the system, the polarizing concentration—by means of surplus-value extraction—of wealth and poverty in the society, the rivalry among capitals and their respective states, and the artificial scarcity that plagues our societies. The reign of value production is also behind capitalism's underrecognition and yet exploitative appropriation of non-value generating care and domestic labor. By contrast, it is only by throwing off the rule of value, by resorting instead to *directly social and hence non-alienated labor,* that people can begin to march not to the rhythms of the law of value, but to the tune of their own drummers, freely working for their mutual benefit.

And, indeed, this is what we have seen in many communes in Venezuela. Here there is a glimmer of light at the end of the tunnel. Even if far from complete, the small index of separation that these communes have opened from the straitjacket of value production has freed the activities and lives of their members enough from its grip to release their human potential in innumerable ways. It is what allows the communards at Che Guevara Commune, where there are no bosses, to exchange activities rather than products, as they do during their Volunteer Work Mondays. It is also what allows the Luisa Cáceres communards in Barcelona, when not engaged in the trash collecting and recycling that is their mainstay, to maintain an urban garden, create colorful planters, and to open a women's center, even though none of these are income-generating activities. In effect, the communal environment provides a framework for breaking with value production and the dictatorship of the market. The communal context allows people to deal and work with each other directly—if not always literally face to face—at least with an awareness of the other's needs and desires, which is the essential step in having production and consumption brought together, and thereby rescuing us from the senseless, anonymous profit-making that is the destructive norm in our society.

The concrete and visible expressions of such emancipation, as varied as they are, are all evidence of this deeper transformation, which enables them. The new rules of the game mean that democratic planning and debate can trump capitalist economic imperatives. For example, when the communards at Cinco Fortalezas worked to move away from sugar production, even though it was more profitable, to food crops like peanuts, or those in El Panal and Che Guevara communes began to develop schooling and care for the old and the sick as in the former's *Club de abuelos*, it was because all these things were determined to be humanly valuable—planned and debated in the communes internal democracy—even if they are not economically valuable. But this could only be done if the commune's self-managed organization of labor is what decides people's activities, not the needs of the capitalist market.

The stakes are high in all of this, the prize being nothing other than human emancipation and planetary survival. The hypothesis of communal socialism is that only by overcoming the rule of blind value production in favor of concrete communal realities and use-values can human beings recover agency and dignity. In our current situation, value-producing time counts as everything and the human being as nothing, as Marx said in his early *Poverty of Philosophy,* adding that, in such circumstances, the human being becomes merely "time's carcase."[5] It is in the commune, then, that the human being can escape the straitjacket that is production time—human time dominated by the dictates of value production—and begin to allocate time according to collectively determined desires and goals.

STATE OF THE COMMUNES

There is still much to be done in this sense. The functioning of the communes in Venezuela remains far from perfect, and many hierarchies still exist. Our trips throughout the country have revealed some of the problems still to be resolved. One of the most important among these is the need to move toward the socialization of domestic labor and the labors of care, to overcome the separation between the social-reproductive domain from other, more visible labor activities that is typical of societies dominated by the capital system. This is still a long way from being realized in most communes, though there have been steps, most of them relatively spontaneous, toward socializing the tasks of social reproduction. Positive measures such as grassroots forms of social security, free neighborhood canteens, schooling, and communal care for the sick and elderly all point in the right direction, while in the Communard Union, and particularly in its member organization, the 5 de Marzo Commune, there is an incipient discourse about communal feminism, focused on promoting women's leadership.[6] But the essential economic basis of patriarchal oppression, namely its contradictory reliance on underrecognized, unpaid domestic and care work, which is usually carried out by women, is still far from being undone in most communes.

Alternatives need to be built to socialize, redistribute, and modernize this work in Venezuelan communes, bringing it to the same level of visibility and efficiency as the communes' other "more productive" activities with which it should be ultimately integrated. Nevertheless, one can be relatively sanguine about the possibilities for the communes to make these improvements and corrections, along with addressing other limitations, provided they maintain a lively internal democracy. Internal democracy allows for self-critique and correction in emancipatory processes that are incomplete because they are laden with baggage from the past. It is likely for this reason that Chávez said, in the *Golpe de Timón* discourse, that the yardstick for socialist progress is substantive democracy, while he worked constantly to develop people's "socialist mass consciousness" in his educational programs.[7] For, as long as grassroots democracy is maintained and applied to problems as they emerge, and there is widespread socialist consciousness inside the communes, then most internal (residual) problems can be worked out. Internal democracy with spaces for debate and reflection provides an effective framework for correcting the course and going forward.

The other loose thread is one that is not so easily solved by internal practices of democracy and self-critique. This is the relation of the communes to the Venezuelan state and their access to the crucial resources it manages. As we have pointed out, in relation to El Maizal Commune (see chapter 1), one of the distinctive historical features of Chavismo is the dialectical relation it has established between grassroots forces, on the one hand, and sometimes sympathetic state institutions, on the other. As against more radically autonomist approaches, such as that of contemporary Zapatismo in Mexico, the Chavista project has demonstrated the essentially positive relationship that can be established between popular power, as a site for developing a new, non-alienated social metabolism, and the sympathetic state apparatus that can result from revolutionary political intervention. This formula has led to unprecedented efflorescences of popular power. Further, an extended period of dialectical coexistence between popular power and the state's institutions is virtually dictated by the situation that Mészáros identified when he showed that no single element of the capital system's triad of *wage labor, state power,* and *capital* can be brought down by decree, but rather the new social metabolism operating in the communes must spread through the society—ideally under an improved configuration of state power—and eventually cause both the state form and the rule of capital to entirely disappear.

The state is not going to go away in the short or middle term, but it can't be ignored either, meaning that, during this extended time of "dual power" coexistence the communes will find themselves struggling with the state to obtain economic and political support—or "disputing state power," as Venezuelan revolutionaries like to say.[8] This task is especially important given the precarious economic situation of most communes in Venezuela and the weakness of the communal movement as a whole. Many of the communes are just surviving on the margins of the country's still largely capitalist economy, while the most pervasive attitude of the communard bases is one of mere resistance. This may constitute an acceptable beginning, but it is not enough. As we implied in chapter 2, in our discussion of the relation of historical communes to modernity, communes must go beyond mere survival and resistance, for the strategic goal is to abolish the entire capitalist economy and generate rich, multifaceted well-being for members of their communities and qualitative human development: to be true matrixes of human emancipation. The latter is what Marx highlighted when he wrote about the need to generate a "realm of freedom" beyond the "realm of necessity," where the struggle for mere existence still operates. Therefore, during the socialist transition, it is necessary that the communes maintain not only their emancipatory social metabolism and internal substantive equality but that they also update and technify some of their production processes, while extending the emergent social metabolism laterally into the society.

The need to go beyond mere resistance and hegemonize the society has the important practical consequence that while the communes will have to struggle to obtain finances and other resources, they must do so in a way that increases their autonomy rather than making them clients. Leaving aside the limited possibility that communes can lean on or "tax" businesses in their respective areas (which is surely done on a small scale, even if it is not legally sanctioned), the main injection of economic resources will have to come from the state, which manages the oil rent. The Venezuelan state, then, is the logical source of what was called in the past "primary socialist accumulation."[9] In this sense, the Venezuelan communes today—even more so because of the renewed interest that is now coming from the president, ministers, and society-at-large—would seem to be likely beneficiaries of the "economic recovery" that is sweeping through the country (see chapter 7). In principle, too, the Communard Union is well positioned to mediate the relationship with the state. However, the inchoate character of the Union means that the relation between state and communes continues to be defined by improvisation, and instead of a clearly defined strategy in the communal movement, there is rather an unpredictable sequence of sallies, parries, and reconciliations. There are offensives and counter-offensives, pushes and pulls, between the two sides. For example, the government has responded to the formation of the Communard Union by developing the "communal economic circuits" project, which represents an alternative pole to the Union that is closer to the ministry. Meanwhile, the executive branch has opened a new can of worms, which offers possibilities for both advancing and retreating, by proposing to reform the *Popular Power Laws*, which include the laws relating to communes.

There are always political dimensions to this contested relation with the state. Yet, even if interesting political debates have emerged, such as the one about the "Communal State," the question of economic support remains the central issue.[10] From the ranks of the communards, one proposal to normalize the state's financing of communes has come forward, which is that 5 percent of the national budget should be dedicated to communes, along with the creation of special *communal economic zones*. An alternative proposal, which is less promising because it is more legalistic, advocates incorporating communes into the Bolivarian Constitution. Clearly the struggles to secure the resources for "primary socialist accumulation" (in its current communal iteration) need to go on. The relation cannot be left to the good intentions of state officials, if for no other reason than that the state currently seems to prefer supporting capitalist development in the country—development led by what it calls "entrepreneurs" and the "revolutionary bourgeoisie." Political pressure from the communes through street campaigns and sectoral lobbying might make the attitude of the state more amenable and perhaps sway the balance to the communal pole of development in a way that would afford sufficient resources for facilitating the new communal metabolism's extension to the whole society, displacing the capitalist sector entirely. Only this, in the end, is what could provide the basis of not just a "friendlier" state—and not just the end of the actually existing neo-colonial state form—but also the abolition of the alienated state form altogether.

A SOLID STARTING POINT

It is all open territory: the future of the communal movement in Venezuela is uncertain, though one can be sure that its destiny is tied to numerous continental and international developments, including the outcome of social and political struggles in Europe and North America, the evolution of the New Cold War, the ongoing project of South-South solidarity, and the future steps taken in the formation of an environmental proletariat that could link worker and ecological struggles across the world. The single most promising thing about the commune, however, is the solid beginning point that it represents. In this sense, it is relevant to return to the question of the "Archimedean point" and the theme of irreversibility that Mészáros put on the table in relation to the socialist transition. For Mészáros, the strategic issue of having a solid starting point, comparable to the one the Greek mathematician imagined could leverage the universe, was posed by the need to find a way out of the vicious circle that the self-positing capital system represents.

In the 1867 preface to *Capital*, Marx wrote that "every beginning is difficult." He was, of course, talking about the exposition of his book and of scientific work more generally. However, he could have extended the principle to other areas. For it is true that beginnings are usually critical in defining what comes next, not only in socialist books but also in socialist movements. The left has gotten off to too many false starts and has pursued too many chimerical approaches to emancipation, as it did in social democracy and state socialism, to take two key examples of powerful movements with bad starting points. These projects, in accepting capital's rules of the game and pursuing a line of least resistance, proved easy to roll back. There was no traction, or the traction they had was too weak. By contrast, the communal movement has the benefit of a solid underpinning. Its solidity is based on how the communes solve a central problem, essentially the Gordian Knot of socialism, which did not have to wait for Chávez or Mészáros to identify it. It was located by Marx himself in one of his early theoretical documents.

The Gordian Knot I am referring to is the puzzle of how a new, socialist dynamic can emerge in what seems to be a closed capital system. Marx addressed the problem in his "Theses on Feuerbach"—written when he was twenty-seven—where he argued that the "educator must also be educated." This statement, which is somewhat cryptic, deals with the question of making a new beginning inside a closed system, doing so by way of a critique of utopian socialism. Utopian socialists such as Robert Owen, Charles Fourier, and Henri de Saint-Simon, also wanted to break out of the vicious circle of capital—the circle in which the activity of most agents is determined by the system's categories—but they proposed doing so by way of preordained, externally imposed plans. Hence, in Marx's lexicon, the utopian socialists felt they were "educators who needed no education," because they already possessed plans from on high. However, Marxism bars appeal to this position because it understands such a God's-eye point of view to be impossible. The critique must be immanent to the system, and the change it pursues must likewise be one that fulfills the double criteria that (1) it emerges from its internal dynamics but (2) nevertheless reaches outside. Failing to fulfill the second of these criteria, one would be accepting the internal rules of the game, practices such as wage labor and the law of value, which is what social democracy and the Soviet system did, albeit in different modalities, thereby repeating the same logic of the capital system, which, in the end, always leads to *culs de sac*, even with these hybrid systems.

Marx proposed another option, a *tertium datur*, or third position, in this conundrum, which is neither the *deus ex machina* solution of the utopian socialists nor the complacency with capital's logic embodied in twentieth-century socialist movements, both Soviet-inspired and social democratic. In fact, the only way to carry out a transformation from the inside and yet do so in a way that points to the outside, via an emergent dynamic, is through revolutionary human praxis. Because of the new consciousness and capacities it generates, human praxis is what can allow us to get a solid foothold and go forward. The solid foothold that is generated by praxis is neither imaginary nor immaterial but directly connects to how labor activities, inasmuch as they are self-determined, create not only new products and services but also new human beings with new emergent characteristics—the *second product of labor*, in Michael Lebowitz's terminology.[11] This second product is nothing other than the new revolutionary or communal beings who operate with different values and practices that, even if born in a capitalist context, represent a radically antithetical logic and alternative social metabolism to that of capital. It is this new logic or dynamic that we can see emerging in communes, as well as in the voluntary labor practices that the Productive Workers Army, following Che's lead, is carrying out with its work brigades (chapter 7). It is the foothold or Archimedean point that allows the communal movement in Venezuela to go forward while avoiding the dead ends and stalemates represented by earlier models of socialist transformation that repeated, in hybrid form, the old capital logic.

It is essentially for this reason that the communal project in Venezuela, however small and however embattled it may be, represents such an important hope for the world. This is because it constitutes a solid and coherent beginning. It therefore has a high degree of irreversibility and offers an example that could be emulated in other parts of the world. Right now, there is a worldwide struggle over the commons, partly based on how new, flexible forms of accumulation, through platforms, financial innovations, and instruments of what has been called "surveillance capitalism," suction value and resources from activities in informal gray zones far outside of workplaces. Targets include the spontaneous affective and intellectual activity on social networks, communal spaces, and even work for social change, for the capital system never ceases to be flexible and creative in its attempts to accumulate in altered circumstances.[12] However, the communes, as they operate in Venezuela, have the distinction of being places where there is a new logic operating based on people living out substantive democracy. They are places where people are freed to live by their own lights and realize their potential in a way that is compatible with others' development and with survival of the Earth system because it opens a window on an emergent logic, overflowing the existing one, that is more human and more sustainable, centering on life rather than value production. Therefore, the communes are also places where those who have surveyed the ruins of history, looking back from a position that takes in the whole, like Benjamin's angel, can stop the ongoing ruin, pull the emergency brake, and begin to build!

Notes

Introduction

1. Karl Marx, *Capital*, vol. 1 (London: Penguin, 1976), 477–79. For information on India, Marx relied on colonial officials such as Mark Wilks, George Campbell, John Budd Phear, and Henry Sumner Maine, as well as Russian anthropologist Maxim Kovalevsky. He tended to either filter out or criticize the racism and Eurocentrism that contaminated these sources, doing so more consistently and more aggressively over time.

2. The sketch here of precapitalist communal production draws on the *Formen* section of Marx's *Grundrisse*. See Karl Marx, *Grundrisse: Foundations of the Critique of Political Economy*, trans. Martin Nicholas (London: Penguin Books, 1973), 471–513, https://www.marxists.org/archive/marx/works/1857/precapitalist/index.htm.

3. Marx, *Capital*, vol. 1, 926.

4. Community production was often followed by other modes of production, such as the tributary, ancient–classical, or feudal modes, before issuing into the capital system. However, these production modes tended to retain some elements of the communal systems, especially embeddedness of workers in labor conditions.

5. Capitalism indeed breaks down many barriers inherent in earlier social formations. However, today it is abundantly clear that some boundaries to expansion and growth must be preserved in the interest of maintaining planetary equilibriums, though the approach to living within such boundaries should be democratically determined, to guarantee fairness.

6. To say that capitalism opens up certain horizons of human development (highly unequally and most often more as possibilities than realities) is not to justify colonialism, which is unjustifiable and is always more damaging than beneficial to the colonized society. People who try to justify colonialism as a bearer of the positive features of capitalist modernity forget that noncapitalist societies, the members of which are just as curious and creative

as members of capitalist ones if not more so, can and do learn from and appropriate specific features of capitalist societies, without being dominated by them and without thereby becoming capitalist (just as capitalist societies have appropriated features and knowledge from other societies). In fact, Marx proposed just this when he argued that the Russian peasant commune, as a fulcrum for socialist construction, could employ certain features of capitalist modernity without passing through a capitalist stage of development.

7. Patriarchal and other forms of oppression are minimal or non-existent in many Indigenous communal societies. However, they become more acute whenever these latter are supplanted by class–based societies, such as tributary and feudal ones, which tend to retain many features of embedded communal production. Needless to say, capitalism is profoundly racist and patriarchal, appropriating and intensifying earlier forms of racial and patriarchal oppression in ways that are functional to surplus labor extraction and to the practices of expropriation that it requires.

8. Living under the capital system forever is not possible, if for no other reason than that it is incompatible with the planetary bases of life.

9. In the *Economic and Philosophic Manuscripts of 1844*, Marx writes of how the laborer's "activity is turned against him, independent of him, and not belonging to him." Karl Marx and Frederick Engels, *Collected Works* (New York: International Publishers, 1975), vol. 3, 275.

10. In English, this connection is barely maintained. However, it is preserved in the archaic word "travail," meaning both difficult work and hardship or suffering.

11. These transformed conditions of communal existence, in which the goal becomes human life and human development, not profit, are sometimes described in Venezuela by terms and slogans such as *vivir viviendo* (to live living), *buen vivir* (good living), and *economía para la vida* (economy for life).

12. See Hugo Chávez Frías, *El libro azul* (Caracas: MINCI, 2013). In this brief book from 1991, Chávez argues for popular democracy and participation, contrasting it with representative democracy.

13. Hugo Chávez, "Strike at the Helm," *MR Online*, April 1, 2015. The discourse was originally delivered in October 2012, https://mronline.org/2015/04/01/strike-at-the-helm.

14. Karl Marx and Frederick Engels, *The German Ideology*, 1845, in Karl Marx and Frederick Engels, *Collected Works* (New York: International Publishers, 1975), vol. 5, 49, https://www.marxists.org/archive/marx/works/1845/german-ideology.

15. Throughout the book, I use the words *socialism* and *communism* interchangeably.

16. Karl Marx and Frederick Engels, *Collected Works* (New York: International Publishers, 1976), vol. 6, 506; Karl Marx, *Capital*, vol. 1, 171, 173; Karl Marx, *Capital*, vol. 3 (London: Penguin, 1981), 568 (twice), 571, 572, 743, 759.

17. Translation modified to reflect the fact that the original word, "Menschen," means *people* or *human beings*, not *men*, as it is often translated.

18. Marx, *Grundrisse*, 171, 591, 882.

19. Marx also said about the Paris Commune that it was "the lever for uprooting the economical foundations upon which rests the existence of classes and therefore of class rule" and described the commune as the "political form of social emancipation." Karl Marx and Frederick Engels, *Collected Works* (New York: International Publishers, 1986), vol. 22, 334, 490, 506.

20. Marx's rejection of state socialism is evident in his *Critique of the Gotha Program*, 1875, where he first openly took distance from a "Marxist" tendency. Karl Marx, *Critique of the Gotha Program* (Oakland: PM Press, 2022), 56-7.

21. In a May 1843 letter to Arnold Ruge, Marx defines the subject of the revolution as including "suffering mankind which thinks" or "suffering human beings, who think." Karl Marx and Frederick Engels, *Collected Works* (New York: International Publishers, 1976), vol. 3, 141.

22. Venezuela's democratic culture owes a great deal not only to the region's egalitarian Indigenous societies but also to the revolutionary rebellion that swept through the country in 1813-14, when members of the Black and Brown majority in the country, led by Asturian *caudillo* José Tomás Boves, successfully ran the white aristocracy out of the Venezuelan territory and leveled its colonial institutions. Steve Ellner, *Rethinking Venezuelan Politics: Class, Conflict, and the Chávez Phenomenon* (London: Lynne Reiner, 2008), 1-50.

23. Reinaldo Iturriza, *Chávez lector de Nietzsche: escritos para atravesar el desierto*, unpublished manuscript, 2017.

24. Hugo Chávez, quoted by Iturriza in *Chávez lector de Nietzsche*.

25. The term "Jetztzeit" that Benjamin uses came from Karl Krauss, and it literally means "a time of the now." It refers to a time of revolutionary possibilities. See Chris Gilbert, "Walter Benjamin in Venezuela," *Monthly Review* 69, no. 5 (October 2017): 15-30, for a discussion of Benjamin's historiography in relation to the Bolivarian Process.

26. Margaret Benston, "The Political Economy of Women's Liberation," *Monthly Review* 17, no. 4 (September 1969): 13-27; Lise Vogel, *Marxism and the Oppression of Women: Toward a Unitary Theory* (Leiden/Boston: Historical Materialism, 2013). More recent contributions to social reproduction theory include Tithi Bhattacharya, ed., *Social Reproduction Theory: Remapping Class, Recentering Oppression* (London: Pluto Press, 2017) and Susan Ferguson, *Women and Work: Feminism, Labour, and Social Reproduction* (London: Pluto Press, 2020).

1. Red Current, Pink Tide: El Maizal Commune

1. See *Aló Presidente Teórico No. 1*, on the todochavez.gob.ve website.

2. In September 2022, Prado won the election for mayor of Simón Planas township, and had his victory recognized.

2. The Long Roots of Venezuela's Communal Tradition

1. Karl Marx, *The Eighteenth Brumaire of Louis Bonaparte* (1852). Karl Marx and Frederick Engels, *Collected Works* (New York: International Publishers, 1979), vol. 11, 206.

2. Peter Hudis, *Marx's Concept of the Alternative to Capitalism* (Leiden/Boston: Historical Materialism, 2012), 177.

3. José Carlos Mariátegui, *7 Ensayos de Interpretación de la Realidad Peruana y Otros Escritos* (Caracas: El perro y la rana, 2010).

4. Ibid., 77.

5. The *ayllu* is a self-sustaining traditional Indigenous commune in the Andean region.

6. Michael Löwy, "Marx, Engels y el Romanticismo," *Marxismo Crítico,* marxismocritico.com/2015/12/14/marx-engels-y-el-romanticismo.

7. José Carlos Mariátegui, "Aniversario y balance," in Mariátegui, *Ideología política y otros escritos* (Caracas: El perro y la rana, 2010), 270.

8. For more information on the late Marx's approach to the Russian commune, see Theodor Shanin, *Late Marx and the Russian Road: Marx and the Peripheries of Capitalism* (New York: Monthly Review Press, 1983); Kevin B. Anderson, *Marx at the Margins: On Nationalism, Ethnicity and Non-Western Societies* (London: University of Chicago Press, 2016); Marcello Musto, *The Last Years of Karl Marx: An Intellectual Biography* (Stanford: Stanford University Press, 2020).

9. See Lawrence Krader, ed., *The Ethnological Notebooks of Karl Marx* (Assen: Van Gorcum & Co., 1974).

10. Marx quoted in Shanin, *Late Marx and the Russian Road*, 17.

11. Mario Sanoja, *Los hombres de la yuca y el maíz: Un ensayo sobre el origen y desarrollo de los sistemas agrarios del nuevo mundo* (Caracas: Monte Avila, 1982), 148.

12. Originally used in hunting, fishing, and farming contexts, the Indigenous term *cayapa* now refers to a wide variety of cooperative work undertakings, similar to barn-raising efforts.

13. Iraida Vargas Arenas and Mario Sanoja Obediente, *La larga marcha hacia la sociedad comunal: Tesis sobre el socialismo bolivariano* (Caracas: El perro y la rana, 2015), 51, 278–79.

14. Vargas and Sanoja, *La larga marcha*, 63–65; Vargas and Sanoja, interview with the author, Caracas, October 2021. Enrique Salvador Rivera argues for the importance of African communal traditions in forming the project of the Coro rebellion in his "The Political Economy of Anti-Slavery Resistance: An Atlantic History of the 1795 Insurrection at Coro, Venezuela," PhD diss., University of California Los Angeles, 2019.

15. José Marcial Ramos Guedes, *Contribución a la historia de las culturas negras en Venezuela colonial*, vol. 1 (Caracas: El perro y la rana, 2018), 45; and vol. 2, 190–200.

16. Edilia Sarmiento de Uzcátegui, *San Juan Bautista de Urachiche* (Urachiche: Alcaldía de Urachiche, 2002), 98.

17. A wonderful expression of the continuity of struggles comes from German Prado of the Alí Primera Commune in Urachiche: "Ours is a campesino organization and, for centuries, we have been struggling so that the land would go back to those who work it. . . . That is why—with the Indigenous peoples who resisted the Spanish empire, with the campesinos who fought with Zamora, and with the guerrilleros who left their footprints in our mountains—we continue to struggle with the oppressed." Cira Pascual Marquina and Chris Gilbert, "The 'Old-Yet-New': Past and Present Intermingle at the Hugo Chávez and Alí Primera Communes," *Venezuela Analysis,* January 13, 2023.

18. Other important *cumbes* were that of Andrés López del Rosario, or *Andresote*, founded in 1732 in the valley of the Yaracuy River, and the Cumbe de Ocoyta in Barlovento, Miranda State, formed by Guillermo Rivas between 1768 and 1771. For more information on Venezuelan *cumbes,* or Maroon communities, and the important role of women including Josefina Sánchez and Manucha Algarín in forming them, see Jesus "Chucho" Garcia, *Afrovenezolanidad e inclusion en el proceso Bolivariano* (Caracas: El perro y la rana, 2018), 23–40.

19. Hugo Chávez, *Aló Presidente Teórico No. 1*, todochavez.gob.ve.

20. John Bellamy Foster has pointed out that "original expropriation" is a term that Marx preferred to the terms "original accumulation" or "primitive accumulation" used by classical liberal political economists. See the discussion in John Bellamy Foster and Brett Clark, *The Robbery of Nature* (New York: Monthly Review Press, 2020), 35–63; and John Bellamy Foster, "Extractivism in the Anthropocene: Late Imperialism and the Expropriation of the Earth," *Science for the People* 25, no. 2 (Autumn 2022).

21. By saying that the project of building socialism is a "universal" one, I do not mean that it is homogenous and even less so that the "universal" can be extrapolated from a specific European, white, or male subjectivity, but simply that the project of building a variant of socialism has become relevant to everyone through the global (universal) spread of capitalism.

3. A Commune Called "Che": A Socialist Holdout in the Venezuelan Andes

1. See Vladimir Acosta, *Reformas liberales y acumulación originaria en América Latina: Colombia y Venezuela en el siglo XIX* (Caracas: Universidad Central de Venezuela, 1989), 388–91.

2. Lenin's slogan from 1920 was "Communism is Soviet power plus the electrification of the whole country."

3. Hyman Minsky, *Stabilizing an Unstable Economy* (New York: McGraw-Hill, 1986), 79.

4. Mészáros and Chávez: The Philosopher and the *Llanero*

1. István Mészáros, *Beyond Capital: Toward a Theory of Transition* (New York: Monthly Review Press, 2000), 680–82.
2. Oliver Ressler and Dario Azzellini, *5 Factories: Worker Control in Venezuela* (2006), 81 min., ressler.at.
3. Jorge Giordani, conversation with the author, Caracas, Venezuela, February 11, 2022. All subsequent references to Giordani's life and his relation with Chávez derive from this interview.
4. *Todo Chávez*, todochavez.gob.ve.
5. Mészáros, *Beyond Capital*, 108–9.
6. Mészáros, *Beyond Capital*, 615.
7. Mészáros, *Beyond Capital*, 108–9.
8. Hugo Chávez, *Aló Presidente Teórico No. 1*, Todo Chávez, June 6, 2009.
9. A high point is Marx's 1857–58 *Grundrisse* manuscript, which contains ample reflections on communal production, consumption, and property.
10. Mészáros, *Beyond Capital*, 131.
11. István Mészáros, "The Communal System and the Principle of Self-Critique," *Monthly Review* 59, no. 10 (March 2008): 33–56.
12. István Mészáros, "The Communal System and the Principle of Self-Critique." Marx himself writes about "communist *mass* consciousness."
13. Ricardo Antunes, introduction to István Mészáros, *The Structural Crisis of Capital* (New York: Monthly Review Press, 2010), 21.
14. Mészáros, *Beyond Capital*, 470.
15. Mészáros, *Beyond Capital*, 472.
16. Mészáros, *Beyond Capital*, 495.
17. Mészáros, *Beyond Capital*, 493.
18. Mészáros, *Beyond Capital*, 676–77.
19. V. I. Lenin, "One of the Fundamental Questions of the Revolution," in V. I. Lenin, *Collected Works*, vol. 25 (Moscow: Progress Publishers, 1977), 370–77.
20. Mészáros, *Beyond Capital*, 491.
21. Mészáros, *Beyond Capital*, 494.
22. Mészáros, *Beyond Capital*, 495.
23. Mészáros contrasts the imposed "division of labor" to the consciously planned "organization of labor." In the latter, workers themselves allot time to different productive tasks according to self-determined criteria. Mészáros, *Beyond Capital*, 757.
24. Mészáros, *Beyond Capital*, 495.
25. Hugo Chávez, "Strike at the Helm," *MR Online*, April 1, 2015, https://mronline.org/2015/04/01/strike-at-the-helm.

5. Three Communes in the East

1. E. P. Thompson, "The Moral Economy of the English Crowd in the Eighteenth Century," *Past & Present* 50 (February 1971): 76–136.

2. "Rentier state" is a term used for states that receive most of their revenues from rents, often those derived from local natural resources. However, it should be pointed out that imperialist countries also rely heavily on rents, especially monopoly rents, which means that it is unfair to criticize economies such as Venezuela's as "rentist" by contrasting them with the "healthy" productive economies of the Global North. More importantly, the oil resource, since it is a limited one that is unevenly distributed on the planet, will inevitably generate rents in a global capitalist economy. The question is who will capture them. It is far better that a dependent country capture its oil rents than that they fall into the hands of the North's multinationals.

3. Fernando Coronil, *The Magical State: Nature, Money, and Modernity in Venezuela* (Chicago: University of Chicago Press, 1997).

4. István Mészáros, *Beyond Capital: Toward a Theory of Transition* (New York: Monthly Review Press, 2000), 761.

5. Tellingly, Robinson Crusoe's independence exists more in the heads of economists than in reality. On the one hand, Robinson himself is aware of the importance of his tools (accumulated labor) and other supplies that connect him to the work of others. On the other hand, after some twenty years on the island, he encounters an Indigenous person ("Friday") and, in typical settler-colonialist fashion, enslaves him. See the interesting article by Stephan Hymer, "Robinson Crusoe and the Secret of Primitive Accumulation," *Monthly Review* 23, no. 4 (September 1971).

6. Sidney Mintz points to the industrial character of the plantation economy, while also highlighting how an early crisis of care created by the factory regime—working parents having less time to devote to meal preparation—played a role in increasing sugar consumption. Sidney Mintz, *Sweetness and Power: The Place of Sugar in Modern History* (New York: Penguin Books, 1986), 74–76, 169–70.

7. Fernando Ortiz, *Contropunteo cubano del tabaco y el azúcar* (Caracas: Monte Avila, 1978), 80; Aimé Césaire, *Toussaint Louverture: La revolución francesa y el problema colonial* (Havana: Instituto del Libro, 1987), 41.

8. The condition of being a fossil fuel producer has been essentially imposed on Venezuela. It is simply a fact that the global fossil fuel economy needs to be smashed as soon as possible—it should have been abandoned much earlier—to have any hope of human civilization continuing in upcoming centuries. However, it cannot be asked of a peripheral country in crisis that it take the first step by abolishing fossil fuel extraction and use alone. (Doing so unilaterally and without support from richer countries would be almost suicidal.)

6. The Communard Union and Its Foundational Congress

1. Hugo Chávez, *Aló Presidente Teórico No. 1*, todochavez.gob.ve.

2. *Unión Comunera: Bases Programáticas y Estatutos 2022*, https://fragata.utopix.cc/file/fragata/Biblioteca-utopix/docuemntos-uc.pdf.

3. Argelia Laya (1926-1997) was an Afro-Venezuelan educator, women's rights activist, Communist Party member, and *guerrillera*.
4. The Communal Economic Circuits are a project initiated by Vice Minister for Communal Economy Hernán Vargas. So far, there are thirteen circuits being developed. One of them connects coffee producers in a highland region of Lara State, empowering them by reviving a coffee-processing center. Another involves repairing a lumber mill in Barinas State that will be managed jointly by the state and the local communities, and direct its surplus to solving those communities' problems with infrastructure.

7. The Guayana Region: Communal Practices and Solidarity Brigades among Industrial Workers

1. Andre Gunder Frank, "The Development of Underdevelopment," *Monthly Review* 18, no. 4 (1966): 17.
2. The South Korea "miracle" is one of the preferred counterexamples mustered against dependency theory. However, dependency theory does not argue that the world system is immobile under capitalism, but rather that it is consistently polarized. Moreover, it should be remembered that South Korea's "miraculous" development was partly stoked by the $13 billion in US economic and military aid that it received between 1945 and 1979, roughly twice as much as the United States gave to all the African countries together in that period. The South Korean state, highly controlled from Washington, also waged war against the country's proletariat, suppressing wages, as it pursued planned development that was favorable to US strategic interests in the region.
3. Eduardo Galeano, *The Open Veins of Latin America* (New York: Monthly Review Press, 1997).
4. Che Guevara, "Discurso en la entrega de certificados de trabajo comunista en el Ministerio de Industrias," August 15, 1964, in *Che Guevara: Obras 1957-1967*, vol. 2 (Havana: Casa de las Americas, 1970).

8. El Panal Commune: Seething with Popular Power

1. Friedrich Engels, *The Condition of the Working Class in England in 1844* (Cambridge: Cambridge University Press, 2010), 23-4.
2. To understand Alexis Vive's attitude toward drug dealing in the barrio, it should be considered that drug use and experimentation, which can be harmless and even positive in some contexts, can have extremely negative consequences in Venezuelan barrios. This is because, on the one hand, when people's lives are made precarious by poverty they are often without the information and supportive context with which to experiment with and use drugs safely. On the other hand, drug dealing in the barrios is usually linked to organized crime and social control.
3. Karl Marx, *Capital*, vol. 1, 284.
4. The utility of communal banks is supported by David Harvey's observation

that self-organized economic projects, such as communes or cooperatives, need to develop alternatives outside the sphere of production, including in the areas of finance and commercialization. This observation by Harvey is surely relevant to the project of building communal socialism, though it should be qualified, inasmuch as it applies only to the period of the transition—that is, while a money economy persists in the society-at-large. David Harvey, *A Companion to Marx's Capital*, Volume 2 (London: Verso, 2013), see chap. 7.

5. Karl Marx, *Grundrisse: Foundations of the Critique of Political Economy* (London: Penguin, 1973), Notebook 7, 708.

6. In the *Critique of the Gotha Program*, Marx criticizes Lassalle's claim that workers should get the "undiminished product of their labor." Karl Marx, *Critique of the Gotha Program*, 56–57.

7. Marx, *Grundrisse*, 488; Karl Marx, *Capital*, vol. 2 (London: Penguin, 1978), 199. Emphasis added.

8. See the discussion of the Great Leap Forward in William Hinton, *Shenfan* (New York: Random House, 1983), 206–53.

9. Epilogue: Looking Back, Looking Forward

1. Bolívar Echeverria, *Vuelta de Siglo* (Mexico, D.F.: Ediciones Era), 117–29.

2. Walter Benjamin, "On the Concept of History," in Howard Eiland and Michael Jennings, eds., *Selected Writings*, vol. 4 (Cambridge, MA: Harvard University Press, 2006), 392.

3. The concept of a "real state of emergency" comes from Walter Benjamin's thesis VIII in "On the Concept of History." It should not be forgotten that, in developing the concept, Benjamin was responding to a specific disaster situation: the rise of fascism and Nazi jurist Carl Schmitt's promoting of *Ausnahmezustand* (state of exception or emergency) which implied the suspension of rights and guarantees. Benjamin's specific idea in advocating a "*real* state of emergency" was that instead of seeking merely a return to normality, the proletariat should respond to fascism with drastic revolutionary action.

4. Rebecca Solnit, *A Paradise Built in Hell: The Extraordinary Communities That Arise in Disaster* (New York: Penguin, 2010).

5. Karl Marx and Frederick Engels, *Collected Works* (New York: International Publishers, 1976), vol. 6, 127.

6. The 5 de Marzo Commune has taken some first steps toward collective care of children and has developed workshops and programs addressing sexual and reproductive health and also gender-based violence. Cira Pascual Marquina, "Feminism and the Urban Commune: A Conversation with Anaís Márquez and Andy Hernández," *Venezuela Analysis*, December 16, 2022.

7. Hugo Chávez, "Strike at the Helm," *MR Online*, https://mronline. org/2015/04/01/strike-at-the-helm.

8. The idea that the Bolivarian Revolution represents a situation of dual power was suggested by Geo Maher and later questioned by Jeffery Webber, among others. Dual power, as described by Lenin and Trotsky, is a short-term situation that is not applicable to the Venezuelan process. However, I use the term here merely as a shorthand for the extended coexistence between the new social metabolism and the state apparatus, that must be a part of any socialist transition. For the debate between Maher and Webber, see George Ciccariello-Maher, *We Created Chávez* (Durham, NC: Duke University Press, 2013); and Jeffery Webber, *The Last Day of Oppression, and the First Day of the Same: The Politics and Economics of the New Latin American Left* (London: Pluto Press, 2016).

9. The terms of *primary socialist accumulation* have been inverted in the Venezuelan context because, historically, primary socialist accumulation was about resources being directed *toward* the state, whereas in Venezuela today socialist projects seek resources *from* the state. Eugene Preobrazhensky, *The New Economics* (Oxford: Clarendon Press), 77–146.

10. There is an ongoing debate about the concept of the "communal state," which Chávez used a few times in his last years and entered into the legal framework for the communes. There are various positions regarding this issue. In the bureaucracy, there is a right-wing position, which may render lip-service to the communal movement, but rejects the "communal state" idea outright, contending that Chávez merely wanted to create a welfare state that offers the rule of law and social justice. On the other hand, for part of the communal movement, the goal of the *communal state* has become almost a rallying cry for overcoming the existing Venezuelan state in the name of a more popular state or even the destruction of the bourgeois state. However, these two positions do not exhaust the complete political spectrum. For there is a second leftist position—supported partly by Chávez's apparent retreat from the term before dying—which argues that speaking of a "communal state" is a contradiction in terms, and that, though it is important to intervene in the state by revolutionary means, the work of implementing a communally organized society that will ultimately abolish the state must essentially occur outside the state's institutions. This last position is backed by good arguments and is likely the most scientific one, even if the political objectives pursued by those calling for a communal state are correct ones.

11. Michael A. Lebowitz, *The Socialist Alternative: Real Human Development* (New York: Monthly Review Press, 2010), see chap. 2.

12. Miguel Mazzeo and Fernando Stratta, eds., *¿Que es la economía popular?: Experiencias, voces y debates* (Buenos Aires: Editorial Colectivo, 2021), 27–30.

Index

Vogel, Lise, 32–33
voluntarism, 97, 186–87
volunteer labor, 147–48, 153–54,
186–87; *see also* Productive
Workers Army

wage labor, 13–14, 32, 79, 98–99,
173, 190
Warao people, 58
Wayuu people, 58
working class: agency of, 23–26,
60–62, 194–95; moral economy
of, 107–108; reproductive labor
of, 13, 32–33, 188; wage labor of,
13–14, 32, 79, 98–99, 173, 190;
see also exploitation; surplus labor

Yanomami people, 58
Yaracuy (Venezuela), 39, 62–64
Yare Prison, 161
Year Zero concept (El Panal
Commune), 174–77, 184
yuca, 57–58, 117
Yukpa people, 58
Yugoslavia (self-managed enter-
prises), 46

Zamora, Ezequiel, 30, 61
Zapata, Emiliano, 54
Zapatismo, 189
Zasulich, Vera, 25, 55–56
"Der Zauberlehrling" (Goethe), 14